Furniture

Waterfalls and Bridges

Alex Brown

718 - FIRM 3406
877 286. FIRM
877.286. FIRM

First Printing, 2015

ISBN 978-0-9962285-1-0

Alexander D Brown

PO Box 80908

Rancho Santa Margarita, CA 92688

http://www.alexbrownsongs.com

"When I was a boy, I dreamed of becoming a man. Through this perilous journey, I learned it takes the heart of a child to become the man I was always meant to be."

Alex Brown

CONTENTS

Introduction

It's been over forty years since I experienced what I call my first miracle. There have been many since then, and that's why I'm writing this book. Over the years, my friends and family have heard some of these stories multiple times. A few years ago they began telling me to write them down. I told myself, "This will make a great project for retirement."

I haven't retired yet, but I'm launching on a journey through my past anyway. Initially, I was very excited about this book. My wife Susan and I began jotting down notes and reliving our past. I thought, "This is going to be so much fun!" Then my daughter Lauren read some of my initial writings.

Lauren liked the stories, but felt something was missing. She said something like "Dad, I want to know more about what it was like growing up in your family. Tell me about the struggles and the painful experiences." My reaction was fairly defensive. "Nobody wants to hear the ugly details of my past. They want to hear about the good stuff, the miracles." The truth of the matter is I didn't want to relive those painful memories. Lauren convinced me that a reader needs to know where you've been, before you tell them where you are. If that's what it takes to put things in perspective, I'm okay with it.

I would love to tell you I've been on a straight and narrow path for the last forty plus years, but it's been far from that. I have gone completely off the road, and have taken more than my share of wrong turns. You won't hear me preaching in this book, and you may be surprised by some of what you read. I hope you will enjoy these colorful stories filled with adventure, humor, trial, and triumph.

It is also my sincere desire that you pause and reflect on what they could mean for you.

1 - Broken Dreams and a Fallen Hero

My father grew up in Syracuse, New York. He was the youngest of three boys, in a family of five. His older brothers Neil and Bob were popular guys in high school, who excelled at sports. Everyone expected Bill to follow in their footsteps, but it just wasn't his thing. He idolized his brother Bob, who went off to war just after graduating from high school. Bob was my father's hero. Bill anxiously waited for his big brother to return from the war, but it never happened. Bob was killed in an explosion, while loading munitions onto a fighter plane. My father's hero was gone, and in his own words, "Life was never the same". Bill served in the

Navy, and then attended Syracuse University as an art student. That's where he met Marion.

My mother was born and raised in Trenton, New Jersey. She spent some time in an orphanage after the death of her mother at age seven, and was adopted in her teens by her aunt Agnes. More than anything, she wanted my mother to get a college education. As a professor at Syracuse University, Agnes was able to pull a few strings, and Marion enrolled as an art student. Then along came Bill. It didn't take long for a wedding to follow, and soon there were three. My mother never graduated from college.

Bill eventually landed a job as Art Director for a local TV station. He would come home from work every evening and play the piano in our dining room before dinner. His mood and the music he played can best be described as melancholy. Once dinner was ready and all six kids were seated at the table, things got ugly. My father would begin to knit pick my mother's meal, or the table setting, or anything else that didn't line up with his expectations. If it wasn't my mom, it was my oldest sister Tina or my older brother Chris. My sister Jill was off limits, because she suffered from severe Rheumatoid Arthritis. And so was my younger brother Michael, who was a baby at the time.

Tina wanted to be a nun for a short period during her high school years, and that provided some pretty heated discussions at the dinner table. Chris was an aspiring rock and roll drummer, and the Beatles were leading a revolution in teenage culture. The "crew cut" was out, and longer hair was in. If a guy wanted to look cool, he had to let his hair grow. The clothes got tighter, the skirts got shorter, and parents were losing ground fast. One of my worst memories comes from an incident where my father tied Chris to a pole in the basement. He cut his hair to military length, as punishment for something I can't even remember. I began to wonder, "When is my number going to come up?" That day came sooner than I anticipated.

2 - The Times They Are a Changing

Tina was off to Cornell University in Ithaca, and Chris was soon headed for Cooper Union in New York City. Before Chris left, there was an incident between him and my father that should have offered a clue as to what was coming. My parent's bedroom was in the basement, along with an art studio that was only accessible through an adjacent bedroom. That was Chris's bedroom, which was soon to be mine. My father had a bathroom built in the basement, with an open top shower, and a toilet. One day as Chris was taking a shower, he looked up to find my father peering down at him over the top. There was a loud verbal exchange, and nobody talked about it much after that. I was too young to understand anything sexual at the time.

Looking back, I can recall some pretty odd exchanges with my father, leading up to my teenage years. On several occasions, he tried talking me into going away with him for a weekend. When I asked where we would stay and what we would do, he said we would stay at a motel and just hang out together. He would tell me not to mention it to my mother, or anyone else. I always got the creeps when he proposed one of those trips, and I never did go away with him alone.

I was about thirteen years old when my father called me into his bedroom for a private talk. He gave me an "anything goes" version of the Birds and the Bees, which sounded more like science fiction, than love between two people. He described an erection, a sexual orgasm, and then asked if I had experienced either one. He showed me how to masturbate, and then offered to help with my first orgasm by performing oral sex. It just didn't seem right, so I declined. Then he encouraged me to begin daily masturbation, and told me to let him know when I was "successful." Of course, this was all just between him and me.

The next day, I ran it by a couple of my pals after school. Rick immediately got his Playboy magazine out, and held an impromptu Sex 101 class right there in his basement. Rick's version of the Birds and the Bees was different from my father's. After seeing those Playboy models, I really liked the idea of being with a woman someday. In the days that followed, I obtained a copy of Playboy magazine and began fantasizing about girls. It didn't take long before I was "successful." I still didn't know what to make of my father's version, or why he was so interested in my sexual development. I did know this much; I was attracted to girls. In the weeks and months ahead, my father's motives would become clear. Things were about to change, and not for the better.

3 - A House Divided Cannot Stand

In retrospect, I can see my father had issues that plagued his life. He was torn by conflicting dreams. On one hand, he dreamed of a big happy family right out of a Hollywood movie script like Cheaper by the Dozen or The Sound of Music. He loved those films, and expected his family to follow those scripts. On the other hand, my father had a very different dream. This one was more like a Fellini film, laced with sexual fantasies and artistic imagery. He tried to keep this side hidden from family, neighbors, and coworkers, but eventually it proved too difficult.

As my hormones kicked into gear, my father began making sexual advances toward me. When I failed to oblige, he became frustrated and angry. One day he would seek my sexual affection, and the next day he was a drill sergeant. I never knew which one would show up on any given day. Then he tried another angle. He began to give me privileges almost any fifteen year old would find appealing. I was naïve enough to think they came with no strings attached. He allowed me to stay out late with my friends, smoke cigarettes at home, and drink an occasional beer with the adults. For a while, his sexual advances stopped. I thought my father was offering some sort of compensation for his bad behavior. I was wrong.

The next wave of sexual advances came with reference to my new found privileges. When I still wouldn't capitulate, things got worse. The drill sergeant got louder, and the lover was more pathetic. I was losing respect for my father, and I was losing my mind. If I spilled the beans, our family would go up in smoke. I didn't want to be responsible for that, so I just tried to cope. It was no surprise to me that my parents weren't getting along. After the kids went to bed, they would argue almost every night.

There were frequent arguments between my father and me too. They usually occurred at the dinner table. It was like waiting for the shoe to drop. At some point in the meal, I made a remark, and my father would snap. I was usually prepared, and ready to run for my room in the basement. He would chase me to the top of the stairs, swinging his fists like Popeye, until I threw myself down to the basement. I learned to take that fall like a Hollywood stunt man. I would hasten to my room, hook the tiny door latch, and fume until the adrenaline wore off. On several occasions, I considered charging back up the stairs to let him have it.

One night, he followed me down the stairs and knocked me out with a single punch. When I came to, my mother was bandaging the hole in my lip where a tooth had punctured it. To this day, I'm thankful for the small still voice that spoke calming words of wisdom, and prevented me from unleashing my anger. Without divine intervention, I would likely have spent my life in prison for murdering my father. Things could not go on like this much longer.

4 - The Darkest Hour Is Before the Dawn

My father's sexual advances continued, and the more I refused the more frustrated and angry he became. He was making my life miserable. I wanted out of that situation so bad, I was becoming desperate. I didn't have a car or a license to drive, so I imagined myself hopping a freight train for New York City to live with my brother Chris. That never happened. Then my father made a twisted proposal. He offered to buy beer for me and my friends, if I would allow him to perform oral sex.

In the art studio, which was only accessible through my bedroom, there was a high drafting table facing a small basement window. I told myself, "If I have to endure this abuse, I might as well get something out of it. Maybe then he will finally leave me alone." I took the bait. I wanted the beer up front, before anything took place. And so there I stood, with my arms on that table, staring out the basement window while my father did his thing from underneath. In my mind, I was somewhere else. I only agreed to a limited number of minutes, and when time was up, I was out of there.

I would meet up with my friends, and we would drink that beer. We laughed, told stories, and put on a pretty good buzz. Somehow I thought it would help dull the pain, and make me "one of the guys." When I woke up the next morning, I was disgusted with my father, and with myself. It only took a few of these encounters, before I said "No more." When he realized I would never let that happen again, he was furious. He made my life difficult, but it was better than living with the guilt and the shame.

Shortly after that, something happened that has affected my life for a long time. Out of desperation, my father slipped into my room while I slept and raped me. I was in the middle of a strange dream, when I woke to find him in the act. He withdrew and scurried out of my room like a frightened animal. I was left in a state of shock, and did everything I could to erase that incident from my memory. It didn't work. The dream I was having before I woke up, became a recurring nightmare. I would awake to find myself in a cold sweat, totally confused, for years to come.

I was now a senior in high school. On one of his visits home from college, Chris showed me how to fabricate a student id card. I made one, and found a store that would sell me whatever I wanted. I had money from my after school job at the library, and was able to buy beer and a decent stereo system. The party was on in my bedroom. My parent's relationship had become so dysfunctional they failed to notice or care that my friends and I were drinking down there almost every night. In the morning, I would sleep in and go to school late.

Then one night, my mother woke me up and asked to help her get the family packed and out the door. My father had beaten her within an inch of her life, and she had just returned from the hospital. She had him arrested, and was in great fear of revenge if he made bail. There was no time to waste, and a taxi was on the way. We were headed to the south side of town to stay with our old friends Vic and Dorothy. Vic was a good man, and tried his best to encourage me. He said I should be an example for my brother and sisters. He told me, "Alex, you're the man in this family now." All I knew was that I hated being away from my friends.

Soon enough, the divorce was over and my mother moved out. My younger brother and sisters decided to stay with my father. They weren't aware of the abuse that had taken place over the years, and wanted to stay in the neighborhood. I thought my father would change, now that the courts were involved. I was anxious to continue the party with my friends.

It didn't take long before my father and I started arguing. He was suddenly concerned about my education, and I told him to leave me alone. I had lost all respect for him at this point, and threatened to have him arrested if he so much as looked at me funny. If looks could kill, I would have died right there and then. He left the house to run a few errands, and I moved in with my mother before he came home.

5 - Music to My Ears

A few months before, I started dating a girl named Annie. I confided in Annie about everything. I was in love, and I bet the farm on our relationship to save me from the past. I didn't know it then, but I was desperate to validate my manhood. That was too much pressure for a young girl in high school, and before the end of our senior year she said goodbye. I was devastated to say the least.

One of the things Annie and I shared together was a love for music. She taught me how to finger pick on my acoustic guitar. Before that, all I could do was strum. My musical heroes were the likes of

James Taylor, Carole King, Cat Stevens, and Neil Young just to name a few. They were singer songwriters, who expressed their feelings to beautiful melodies with skillful guitar and piano playing. One listen to Fire and Rain and I was hooked.

I began to write my own songs, in hopes it would ease the pain of a broken family and a broken heart. It wasn't working. I was depressed and feeling hopeless. Then something wonderful happened. On a warm summer night just after sunset, I was alone in my mother's apartment. With the lights turned out, I was contemplating how to end my life. I emptied the medicine cabinet and began arranging a concoction that would solve all my problems once and for all.

At that very moment I was startled by the sound of a telephone ringing on the wall. There was no answering machine to take a message, and who knows how long it would continue to ring. I answered the call. At first I thought it must be a wrong number. I didn't recognize the caller's voice. But it was me he was trying to reach, and after a moment or two I realized who it was. A few weeks earlier, I played some of my songs at a Christian coffee house. That's where I met Werner. After the show, he told me about his relationship with Jesus Christ. It pretty much went in one ear and out the other, or so I thought.

As far back as I can remember, I believed in God, but never made a connection with Jesus. I would often lay awake at night conversing with God about my life. I referred to him as "The Man". Werner was calling to invite me to a concert in Ithaca, N.Y. at a place called The Love Inn. I had no idea who the performer was or what this place was all about, but given the timeliness of his invitation, I accepted.

After a moderate drive, we pulled into the dirt parking lot of what appeared to be a large barn somewhere in the countryside. Inside the barn was a very cozy atmosphere with a kitchen, a bookstore, and a loft where the concerts were held. Tonight's performer was Danny Taylor.

He would be playing acoustic guitar and singing original songs. I don't remember much detail about the songs, but they were melodic, and his voice was very pleasant. What I do remember, is what happened after he stopped singing.

Once the music stopped, Danny began to speak about God's love for us. He talked about Jesus Christ and described a personal relationship with him. His words melted my heart and I began to sense the presence of God like never before. It was warm, and pure, and extremely powerful. I was ready to experience a personal relationship with God. I prayed a prayer in my heart along with Danny Taylor that night and the tears flowed freely from my eyes when I accepted Jesus Christ as my Lord and Savior.

On the drive home, I shared the good news with Werner. I told him what was happening when his phone call interrupted me earlier that evening. He was happy to know God used his timely invitation to save my life. Since then, I've seen these eleventh hour miracles more times than I can count.

6 - A Healing Hand

Soon after that miraculous night, I was invited to attend a special service at a small church near the campus of Syracuse University. The guest speaker was a woman named Roxanne Brant, who was known to facilitate healings after her message.

At the time, I wasn't concerned with obtaining a healing miracle for myself. I did however have a large growth on my left hand, which had been removed a few months earlier. Once removed, it appeared to have deep roots, like tentacles. Then it came back with a vengeance. Just a few days earlier, I had shown it to my mother, and we made plans to consult with the doctor again. I wasn't thinking about my hand when I attended the service that night. I was there to receive a healing "by proxy" for my sister Jill, who was not able to attend. Jill has severe Rheumatoid Arthritis, and has struggled with it since the age of twelve. I was there to obtain a healing for Jill.

After Roxanne delivered her message, she prayed and asked God if there was anyone He wanted to heal that night. She began to speak in very specific terms of a particular person being healed of a particular disease. She would describe each person in a way that they could recognize themselves, all from the pulpit as we sat with eyes closed in a state of prayerful reverence. Then she began to describe a young man who was not there for himself. He was there for someone else, but God was going to heal him instead. This young man has a growth on his left hand, which has not responded to medical treatment. God is healing your hand. I felt a warm and powerful presence throughout my entire being.

When the healings were over and all eyes open, I was afraid to look at my hand. It must have been me she was describing, that much would seem undeniable. Finally, I looked at my hand and there it was. The growth was still there. "Oh well, it's okay" I told myself. God is still good and it must have been meant for another young man.

The next morning came, and I slid out of bed to begin my morning routine. Splashing cool water on my face, I prepared to start the day. Something was different. My hand felt smooth, as it stroked across my face. I toweled the water from my eyes and took a look at my left hand. It was gone! Completely and totally gone! My mother was the first person I showed my hand to that day. She was speechless. I don't know if this had anything to do with my mom coming to know Jesus Christ, but I can tell you that she has had a very personal relationship with Him for as long as I can remember.

7 - A Full Circle

One Saturday morning, I picked up the newspaper in my mom's kitchen and saw a furnished studio apartment for rent on the south side of town, not too far from where I worked at the library. The price was just right for my budget, and it was available for immediate occupancy. It was time to move out on my own. I called the manager and then called my friend Marc for a ride. I had everything I needed to seal the deal when we arrived at the apartment on East Kennedy Street. I approached the manager's downstairs apartment and rang the buzzer. I could hear his wife call for him to see who it was, as I waited outside.

The look on Don's face as he opened the door

was priceless. It was a mix of surprise, disbelief, and humor. As tactfully as he could, Don asked if I had noticed anything different about the area as I approached the building. When I said no, he just scratched his head, smiled, and gave me a nod. After a quick tour of the apartment, I signed the papers and we shook hands. He welcomed me to the neighborhood and offered up some practical advice in regards to anything valuable I might own. Don was a family man, and a very genuine human being. He made me feel at home.

The next few months went along without incident. I rode my Schwinn five speed bicycle to and from work, and carried it upstairs to my second story dwelling every time I arrived. When I wasn't working, I was playing my guitar and writing songs. I shared a common bathroom with another apartment down the hall and there was a guy living right above me who could have passed for the sixties soul singer, Isaac Hayes. Maybe that's why everyone called him Shaft. All in all, I got the feeling everybody was okay with me living there.

I can only think of two occasions where someone in the neighborhood questioned a young white guy, living in an all-black community. One was a young boy maybe twelve years old, sitting on his porch as I walked by one afternoon. He flat out asked me, "What are you doing in this part of town anyway?" I replied sincerely, "The same as you. I'm living here." He seemed to accept that answer and I moved along. The other was late one night as I passed a bar at the corner on my way home. Leaning against the outside wall, the young man said "I know what you're all about. You think your fooling everybody, but you don't fool me." I smiled, wished him a good night, and went home.

As the autumn weather was fast approaching, I agreed to help my friend Geno move his belongings to Oswego State University. After a long drive and too many trips from the car to his dorm room, we decided to take a brief swim in Lake Ontario. This decision would have multiple ramifications for me. First, the lake was very cold. Second, I had no bathing suit. Third, my only key to the common bathroom on East Kennedy was in the pocket of my cutoff jeans. When all was said and done, I was cold, wet, and keyless. I actually went back into the water and attempted to recover my bathroom key. Now I was really cold, really wet, and still keyless.

I told Don about it and paid a twenty five dollar replacement fee. There was only one problem. The building owner wouldn't be on site with my new key until the following weekend. I would have to use a restroom at the gas station down the street. I quickly made friends with the station owner, who empathized with my situation. It was going to be a very long week. At one point, a woman down the hall realized my predicament and offered to share her key with me. The same woman later told me how much she and her family enjoyed listening to me play the guitar and sing. She even invited me to share Thanksgiving dinner with her family. I will never forget her kindness.

Sometime after Thanksgiving, I had an experience that might be described as a vision. I had a very strong sense that I should call it a night early, and go to bed. It was around seven o'clock or so, and I would never have gone to bed that early without being sick. I was compelled to do it. I went to bed and fell asleep, only to wake up in what I would describe as a "half conscious" state. I was aware of everything in the room, but not quite awake. My father appeared at the side of my bed. He was crying, and asked me to move back home. It seemed as though he was actually standing there. The experience was intense to say the least.

When I woke up, I had one prevailing thought on my mind. I need to move back home, and leave on good terms the next time. I called him up, explained what had taken place, and moved back in a few days later. If someone told me that was going to happen a week before, I would have said they were insane. I had no logical explanation for it.

At the time, he had a live in companion. I was completely aware of his relationship with Dell. As it happened, I spent more time hanging out with Dell, than I did with my father. He was likeable, and extremely patient. He spoke candidly about the challenges of living with my father, and appreciated the fact that I could relate. Dell seemed to bring out the best in my father. They both showed support for my fledgling music career, and would often come out to watch me perform. In spite of our rocky relationship, my father always encouraged me to pursue music. Years earlier, he observed me playing air guitar one night. In a rare act of spontaneity, he took me out and bought me a Harmony acoustic guitar. Within a week I learned my very first song and performed it for him as he came home from work. It was Darling Be Home Soon by John Sebastian.

8 - Be Careful What You Ask For

The year was 1972 and I was planning a road trip with my friend Brian to travel from New York to California. The day before our scheduled departure, I received a phone call from my sister Jill, a student at Le Moyne College. She told me about an opportunity to be the opening act for a national recording artist named Steve Goodman. At the time, Arlo Guthrie was enjoying a hit single with Steve's song The City of New Orleans. There was only one catch. The gig was that night and I would have to appear at the college for an audition within the next hour or so.

I didn't own a car, so I grabbed my guitar and headed for the bus without thinking twice. That is, until I was actually on the bus headed for the audition. I began to panic. I could feel my hands shaking and sweat was beginning to form on my forehead. This was crazy! How could I pass the audition let alone perform in front of a paying audience in such a nervous state? I began to pray. Lord, maybe this isn't the career for me after all. If I'm going to do this thing I will need your help. Tell you what Lord, if you want me to pursue this music thing, let this go better than I could imagine. Okay Lord?

Be careful what you ask for. I arrived at the auditorium and met Tony. We shook hands and he said "I'm ready whenever you are. Let's see what you've got". I pulled out the guitar, tuned up, got on stage and just started strumming and singing something I had never even played before. I was improvising on some kind of Hello People Woodstock vibe. After that, I sang a few more songs and Tony said "Sounds great, do you have enough material for a 40 minute set? If you're lucky you might even get an encore. Who Knows? Make sure you save a good one just in case."

I spent the rest of the afternoon with my sister getting a tour of the campus and meeting her friends until the show. Then before I knew it, the time arrived. I heard my name being announced and Tony said "You're on kid, good luck." I broke out with the Hello People thing and it just flowed with ease from there. I sang my songs, and told amusing stories. The audience applauded, laughed, and cheered for more when it was over. I got the encore. The next morning Brian and I headed west in his 1962 Ford Falcon.

9 - Wandering In the Desert

One afternoon we stopped for lunch somewhere in Tennessee. As it happened, the high school principal was also the owner of the diner. He sat down at our table and began to describe a drug problem at his high school. Certain hippie types from up north had been selling drugs to his students. Apparently, we looked just like hippie type drug dealers from up north, with our long hair, beards, and New York plates on the Falcon. We assured him that we were in fact, good mannered Christian boys, on our way to visit family out west. Before he would believe our story, we actually had to quote scriptures and produce our Bibles.

We finally arrived in Phoenix, Arizona where Brian's cousin was living. For the first night, Lance had us sleeping in a tool shed. We drank a few beers and he described the situation. He had just returned from Vietnam, and was having some sleep issues. Basically, he didn't want to risk accidently shooting one of us in the middle of the night. He slept with a gun under his pillow, and was subject to random episodes in which he would wake up and search the house with his loaded gun in hand.

After a few nights, Lance suggested that Brian and I camp out in the desert. It had to be better than the tool shed. We had a tent, and a little money for supplies, so why not. Firewood, matches, stew pot, pinto beans, hot dogs, mustard, ketchup, ice chest, water, beer, and a 1962 Ford Falcon. What more could we possibly need?

We set up camp and removed the back seat of the Falcon to use as a couch. By sundown we were cooking our first dinner over an open flame. Beans and franks with a few cans of Coors to wash it down. Life was good. The next morning Brian decided we should explore our surroundings in the car. He took the wheel with me riding shotgun and proceeded to tear it up. We were flying over dunes and sliding around corners with the greatest of ease. This was fun!

Then he pulled over and told me to take the wheel. He said it was about time I let off some steam. I reluctantly took the wheel and began tooling around in the dirt. That's when I heard these fateful words, "Give it some gas!" I threw caution to the wind and hit the accelerator. It felt pretty good! That is until we found ourselves in a ditch about the size of a 1962 Ford Falcon. We were letting off steam alright, but this time it was coming from the radiator. Brian's car was officially out of commission.

As we hiked back to camp, he did his best to assure me that it wasn't my fault. I was feeling pretty bad. After a few beers, we hiked out of the desert and found a pay phone at the Circle K convenience store. Lance came out and towed the Falcon back to the house, along with Brian and me. The camping trip was over.

10 - Meltdown at the OK Corral

One afternoon, Lance decided that someone had stolen his girlfriend's dog. She was hysterical, and took some Valium to calm her nerves while Lance searched for the missing pet. The scene escalated when he discovered the dog in his neighbor's yard. He proceeded to get his gun and was threatening to take it back by force. She and Brian pleaded with him not to do anything rash. Maybe it was all a misunderstanding.

I got pretty nervous watching Lance pace around with his gun. That's when I decided to head for the bathroom. The bottle of Valium was sitting right there beside the sink. I had never taken anything like that before, but if there was ever a time, it was now. I took two, and proceeded back to the couch. In a matter of minutes, it was like watching a movie. The only thing missing was the popcorn. When all was said and done, nobody got shot, the dog was back, and everyone settled in to watch TV.

I woke up later that night and made a decision. I was leaving in the morning, with or without Brian. The sun rose, and I was ready to roll. I explained my plan and Brian reluctantly agreed to go under one condition. He wanted to head for Santa Monica, California. He was determined to see the ocean. We thanked our hosts, Brian signed the Falcon over to his cousin, and we were on our way.

Before long, we caught a ride all the way to California. There was only one problem; we were not in Santa Monica. We were in Bakersfield, and it was very hot. We must have waited for three hours before I began to crack. I insisted that we turn around and head east. I didn't care about seeing the ocean, and I wanted to go home. After a heated discussion, we were headed east.

Our first ride took us back to Phoenix. Brian suggested we head north to see the Grand Canyon, and then east on US 40. It sounded good to me and I wanted to get out of Phoenix as fast as possible. Before long, we caught a ride to Flagstaff and headed for the Grand Canyon. There were a few hours of daylight left when we got dropped off near one of the park entrances. We were so close, but not quite there.

11 - Adventures in the Wild West

When we stepped out of the vehicle, I knew we
were in trouble. It was February, and we were not
equipped for cold weather. As it started to snow, we
took one look at each other and agreed to get out of
there. We caught a quick ride towards New Mexico,
and a couple of Native American brothers picked us
up. The older was just returning from Vietnam, and
wanted to talk about the war. We had long hair and
beards, so I guess we looked like a couple of hippie
type war protestors. We did our best to assure them
we were not, and that we appreciated what our
servicemen did for the country.

It was getting dark by now, and our new friends insisted we join them around the campfire at one of their favorite drinking spots. They pulled up to a market and purchased a large quantity of beer and firewood. We were in for a long night. As the sun made its final showing, we pulled off the main road and hiked down into a small canyon. The fire was lit and the beer was flowing. The conversation was friendly enough, and they were beginning to lighten up as we shared stories and laughs together.

At one point, they confessed their initial intentions were not so friendly. They patted us on the back, and insisted we keep drinking until all the beer was consumed. We did just that, and after fueling the fire with the remainder of wood, they left us for the night. As the sun rose over that canyon the next morning, I told Brian to look up. There was a pack of Coyotes around the ridge, looking down at us from above.

Springing to our feet, we tossed rocks in their direction, and yelled as they slowly wandered off.

We were pretty hung over, as we hiked out of that canyon back to the interstate. Our next few rides brought us through New Mexico and into a small Texas town. The sun was getting ready to set, and we decided to sleep in a park at the center of town. As we prepared to settle in, a local rancher told us we would never last the night if we didn't move along. He didn't have a problem, but the young cowboys would likely beat the daylights out of us after drinking all night. He was kind enough to give us a ride out of town.

The sun was down, and we were ready to call it a night. That's when we got the ride of our lives. A pickup truck pulled over and motioned for us to hop in the back. We jumped in without a thought and sat across from each other in the truck bed. Before we knew it, our cowboy driver was playing chicken with the oncoming big rigs and running his truck in and out of the ditch along either side of the highway. We hung on for dear life, and he finally pulled over to let us out. Brian was so angry, he pulled him out of the cab to let him have it. Our cowboy was drunk, and just fell to the ground laughing. Eventually he got up and drove off with a wave of his hat.

12 - My Home Town

We stayed awake all night and kept a low profile
after that episode. When morning broke, we began
hitching a ride early. We thought maybe the worst
of the bunch might still be sleeping it off. We were
pretty skeptical, but managed to make our way into
Oklahoma without any trouble. That's when a
young man wearing a cowboy hat pulled over in his
van. He was headed all the way to Indiana, and
turned out to be a pretty nice guy. He had a guitar
with him, and was happy to learn that I could play.
As we pulled off to camp for the night, we played
guitar and sang songs around the campfire. We all
became pretty good traveling pals.

Turns out he had taken a ranch job in Oklahoma, and was headed home to visit his parents. When we arrived at his parents' home, he introduced us as friends and insisted we spend the night. We took showers while his mom washed our clothes, and enjoyed a home cooked dinner with his family. The next morning, his mom cooked up a huge breakfast and he drove us back to the interstate. We couldn't thank him enough for his friendship and hospitality. As if that wasn't enough, he gave us some cash for the remainder of our journey. That was the best ride we had, and the last of our good times on the journey home.

Eventually we made our way out of Indiana and into Ohio. It was getting dark and a bit chilly when we landed our next ride. It was another van, but this group was different. After questioning us for a while, they decided to reveal their situation. They were a band of self-proclaimed gypsies, making their way across the country any way they could. They let us know in advance, they would be siphoning gas, and shoplifting food as they went along.

We travelled with the gypsies until very late that night. They made their way into Pennsylvania, and were in need of gas to go any further. We were given the opportunity to hop out before they got down to business, and we took it. There was only one problem. It was late, we were exhausted, and it was cold. That's three, but the real problem was our attire. We were wearing tee shirts in February.

It turned out to be one the longest nights of my life. Not many vehicles passed by, but each time they did, we tried to flag them down as if our lives depended on it. Not one even stopped to hear our plight. At one point, we literally begged a State Trooper for a ride. He blew us off saying, "Maybe next time you'll be prepared." He was our last hope. We were in for a long, cold, miserable night.

When our first ride of the morning came along, we were frozen stiff. A group of college students in a VW Mini Van came along, and we climbed in without a word. After realizing we were in pretty bad shape, they cranked up the heater as far as they could for the remainder of our ride. They dropped us off just south of Binghamton, New York on interstate 81. This was the road that would lead us home to Syracuse, New York.

Our final ride was a young Syracuse University student. We reminded her of a younger brother who had recently hitched his way across the country with a friend. She couldn't bring herself to pass us by. I don't remember much about that afternoon. I remember being glad that I was home. I remember sitting in the midday sun thinking, "This is my home town."

13 - Working on the Erie Canal

Shortly after returning home, I became friends with David, who eventually became my brother in law. David's father knew a man who worked for the state of New York. Frank managed a project to create what is now called the Erie Canal State Park. David's younger brother Stephen and myself hired on, along with a college graduate named Art. Frank ran the show with his right hand man Don, who owned a horse ranch and a western clothing store which his wife ran. It was quite a diverse crew. A cast of characters you might see in a TV situation comedy.

Frank was British, and had worked as a carpenter for much of his life. He was approaching retirement, and had little tolerance for sloppy workmanship or horseplay. He was a perfectionist, who prided himself on the ability to measure and cut lumber without the use of a measuring device. On the first day of our tenure, he demonstrated this skill to our collective amazement. He would call out a length, make the cut, and then ask each of us to measure the results. He was dead on the money every time.

Art recently graduated from college, and was looking to become a state park ranger. As a student, he had worked at a KOA campground somewhere in Colorado. He told some pretty good stories, as we toiled away on the seemingly infinite canal tow path. Each of us was taught to drive the sixteen speed, dual stick shift, dump truck. You had to double pump the clutch every time you shifted gears, or a loud grinding sound and subsequent repair would ensue. Don was also the crew mechanic, and did not enjoy spending the entire day underneath that old truck if it could be avoided.

Stephen and I were fresh out of high school and had never experienced anything close to hard labor. We were good at clowning around, and that was about all. It didn't take long before we found ourselves wielding axes, chain saws, sledge hammers, drills, tractors, and back hoes. We worked outdoors, in every weather condition imaginable. Spring turned into summer, then fall, and when winter arrived, we were still outdoors. One of the scariest things I remember was driving the dump truck in reverse, on the narrow snow covered tow path for several miles at a stretch. It required a special "mirrors only" driving technique, and nerves of steel. Nobody wanted to slide down the steep banks, into a frozen canal.

I owned a Chevy station wagon, which required a good half hour of warm up time before attempting the drive to work. Sleeping in too late, and dealing with that car, eventually cost me the job. One morning, as I was warming up the engine, an electrical wiring harness decided to melt. The car was finished, and so was my job on the Erie Canal.

14 - California Dreaming

Soon after that, I landed a job at one of the area's largest manufacturing facilities. I applied as a general assembly line worker, and then seized an opportunity for something entirely different. While filling out paperwork, a manager walked into the room and asked if anyone could drive a forklift. I offered my dump truck experience as qualification. There were four of us contending for the job, but only one opening. We were taken out to a storage yard and given a brief course in forklift operation. Each candidate got into his own forklift and we were instructed to move stacks of metal skids from one side of the yard to the other. It was a forklift driving derby. When the dust settled, the job was mine. The only down side, was that the opening was on the night shift.

As it turned out, the union pay scale for a fork lift driver was significantly higher than the rate for an assembly line worker. I didn't own a car, but as it happened, my neighbor worked the same shift and was happy to have a passenger share the cost of gas. It didn't take long before I was able to replace the burned out Chevy wagon with a blue 1967 Dodge Van. On weekends, I customized the van with help from my friend Werner and his cousin Rick. We lined the interior with insulation, wood paneled the inside walls, laid plywood flooring with a blue padded carpet, and finished it off with matching curtains on the windows. When the work was done, that van was my pride and joy.

In the process of customizing my van, Rick and I became friends. He was looking for someone to share an apartment, and I was ready to move out on my own again. Before moving out, I made an attempt to clear the air with my father regarding the sexual abuse I had endured. The conversation was civil, but didn't produce what I was looking for. I wanted my father to apologize, and it never happened. I moved out without any drama, and we remained in touch.

Rick and I found an apartment on the north side of town, in a predominantly Italian neighborhood. We learned to drink espresso, and ate some of the best Italian food I have ever tasted to this day. It was a vibrant neighborhood, with lots of shops and cafes. We had a good stereo system, and a large record collection. Rick worked at the local UPS distribution center, and we had no trouble paying the bills. Things seemed pretty good for a while. Then Rick's girlfriend announced that she and her family were moving to Huntington Beach, California.

It didn't take but one visit to California, before Rick announced he was following suit. I couldn't blame him for wanting to be with his girlfriend, but

I was in a hurry to find another roommate. My income was not enough to pay the bills.

My friend Werner found a temporary solution. Werner's friend Lenny lived with his mother. Lenny was an avid audiophile, and had just purchased a high powered, high tech, quadraphonic sound system. It required four speakers to be placed symmetrically around the perimeter of a room, and a central listening position. There was no such room available at his mother's house, let alone the ability to crank up the volume and enjoy hours of blissful listening. Lenny had a good job, and was willing to rent Rick's old room for his sound system. The only stipulation was that I never go in the room without Lenny being present, and only when invited. Lenny took his listening sessions pretty serious. I agreed, and the quadraphonic sound system moved in.

As time went on, I was really getting tired of the night shift. An opportunity came up to work the day shift as an assembler, and I took it. It was hard to make the adjustment from fork lift driver to assembler, but they assured me I was first in line when a forklift driver position became available. I wore thick rubber gloves, and spent endless hours dipping coil tubes into a solder flux solution. One night after work, my hand was getting numb. I was shocked to see that my left index finger had turned completely white and hard. An investigation revealed a small pinhole leak in one of the rubber gloves, where toxic solder flux had soaked into my hand. I was placed on medical leave and paid workman's comp while being treated. After several weeks of medicinal treatment, I was cleared for work. Upon returning, I was placed on the residential unit assembly line, as an inspector. No more chemicals for me.

After a particularly harsh winter, I decided to use some vacation time and visit Rick in California. I had enough money for airfare, and could stay with Rick at his girlfriend's house for the week. Rick had a job, and he had a car to drive us around in. He took the week off and gave me the royal tour. Hollywood, Disneyland, Mexico, and Newport

Beach. The sun never stopped shining, and the girls were beautiful. My mind was made up. One way or another, I was moving to California someday.

When I returned to my job, fate took me in a new direction. The union called for a strike, and there was no work for several weeks. My savings were dwindling fast, and I decided to look for another job. I wanted something meaningful for a change. I wanted to make a difference in the world, and my music career wasn't exactly taking off. I called my old boss at the library, and she had some ideas.

Sally was a kind woman, with a heart for helping troubled youth. In the past, she had connected me with several youth homes to perform my songs. She knew people in those establishments, and they liked her. It didn't take long, and I was interviewing for the position of resident counselor at a local children's center. The interview went well, and I was invited back for a second meeting with two of the senior resident counselors. That meeting went well, and the job was mine.

15 - Life at the Cottage

The campus consisted of about ten large brick cottages, several common use buildings, and an administrative complex. Each cottage was occupied by a half dozen or so young clients and two resident counselors. The job required week long, twenty four hour a day shifts for each team. Teams would alternate weeks, giving everyone a seven day period in which to regain some measure of sanity before returning to work. Bob and Ted were the senior team for my cottage, and I was initially paired with Donna who was later replaced by Hal.

Bob was a laid back dude straight out of college,

who aspired to be an Olympic swimmer. Ted was a cool cat who grew up on the south side of town. He was a street wise graduate from the school of hard knocks. I don't remember much about Donna, but I remember that she didn't stay on very long. I also remember that she drove a yellow 1973 Chevy Camaro Z28. Hal was a Syracuse University graduate from New York City. He and his girlfriend Debbie planned to live on a Kibbutz in Israel after she graduated the following year. Hal was a minimalist in the truest sense of the word. He liked to travel light, and limited his possessions to the bare essentials.

The young teenage boys living in my cottage were all there for one reason. One or both of their parents couldn't deal with their emotional problems any more. Most were on medications of one sort or another, the most common being Ritalin. Understandably, they all had abandonment issues and found it difficult to trust the adults in their life. There are four boys who stand out in my memory. Joe, Tim, Patrick, and Tony. As personalities go, they were very unique from each other. At times, they would unite for a common cause, like breaking in the new resident counselor.

Joe was a skinny, dark haired, loveable live wire. He had a great smile, and loved to laugh. His clothes were always a little disheveled, with his shirt not quite tucked in and his shoe laces untied. Everything would seem fine for hours, when suddenly Joe would come unglued and begin assaulting the bedroom furniture. It took a great deal of time and patience to talk him down, but when Joe finally cooled off he would give you the hug of your life.

Tim was a handsome, brown haired, soft spoken kid. He was always neatly dressed from head to toe, and had a smooth manner about him. Tim also had a dry sense of humor, and would crack a knowing smile when you finally got the joke. He was a bit moody, and could verbally lash out in anger on occasion. For the most part, we couldn't understand why he was there. His parents would schedule a visit, and sometimes they never showed up. When they did, it became clear Tim wasn't the problem.

Patrick was a short, witty, clever old man, trapped in the body of a teenage boy. He was always up to something, and loved to keep you guessing. Patrick would begin the conversation on a serious note, and just when you took the bait, say something completely off the wall. We were having one such conversation, when he leaned in, looked me straight in the eye, and said "If you see Moses riding on a motorcycle, tell him I said hello." He was also good at organizing the boys to assist him with his latest plot. Whenever the cottage was about to leave on a field trip, we had to conduct a thorough search of the premises to find Patrick's booby trap. It usually involved fire.

Tony was big and tall, with a large afro, and an even larger heart. He was a sensitive, gentle giant who loved to play basketball. He was a local kid, who grew up in an area of town known as the projects. He was fairly quiet most of the time, unless someone pushed him into a corner. During my tenure at the cottage, Tony was a new arrival, and Ted took him under his wing. He made sure the boys gave him space to adjust, and before long he learned to shake it off when they were messing with him. Tony wouldn't hurt a fly, but he gave the impression that you shouldn't push your luck.

By the end of a seven day shift, I was completely fried and exhausted. There were times I considered leaving, but the thought of letting those boys down, and seven days off was enough to keep me coming back for a while. I could see the long term effects in the faces of those who had exceeded their limit. Dave and Janice, a young married couple, had been there for several years. When they finally decided to move on, everyone understood. Several months later during one of their return visits, Dave said he didn't realize how stressed out he was until he left. He felt ten years younger.

As winter began to set in, I started thinking about California. Lenny had just given me notice at the apartment, and already moved his quadraphonic sound system out. He paid enough rent in advance so I could find a roommate or give my notice. That's when my friend Marc invited me to move in with him on the west side of town. I gave a month's notice and booked a week's vacation to visit Rick in California again.

Within a day after arriving in Huntington Beach, my left index finger began to feel strange. Then it started throbbing with a level of pain I knew meant trouble. Rick drove me to the Emergency Room of a local hospital, and they refused to look at it because I couldn't show proof of insurance. This happened again at two more hospitals. I called my father to see if I was covered under his policy, but they still wouldn't treat me without detailed documentation up front. My father urged me to head home as fast as I could, and we were on our way to LAX. On the plane ride back, the pain continued to worsen.

16 - A Close Encounter

My father met me at the airport and rushed me straight to the hospital. When the Emergency Room clerk looked at my hand, she called for a doctor. He took one glance and proceeded to grab my arm and pull me down the hall. When I asked about the paperwork, he said there was no time for that. He then dipped my hand into a solution and gave me several painful injections. He was prepping for surgery. I had no idea what was happening until he was about to make the cut.

He looked at me intently and then smiled, saying "I know you. You're my little brother's friend. You play the guitar, don't you?" I said yes, and he continued. "I'm Tommy's older brother. I went to medical school and now I'm going to operate on your hand. You'll be happy to know, I learned a new technique which will enable you to keep playing guitar! The normal procedure would have permanently left you without any feeling in that finger. By the way, see this line in your arm? That's the poison from your finger, travelling up the vein to your heart. Once it gets past your elbow, you have less than two hours to live. It's at your elbow right now."

He proceeded to install a drain in my finger, and assured me I was going to live. He said I might be in some pain later, and that I should begin taking the prescribed pain meds before leaving the hospital. I took the pill and my father drove me back to the apartment. He stayed around to make sure I was okay, and then I discovered just how much pain one index finger can cause. Before an hour had passed, I was in complete agony. I tried doubling up on the pain meds, but it didn't help. It was getting worse by the minute, and I was going insane. My father called the hospital and convinced them to prescribe something stronger. It seemed like hours before he returned with a bottle of Percodan. I took two instead of the recommended dose of one, and sat in my easy chair writhing in pain for what felt like eternity.

Finally, I was overcome by a calm peaceful feeling, and the pain was gone. I fell asleep and drifted into dream land. The next few days, consisted of Pink Floyd and Percodan. I thank God for using my father and Tommy's older brother to save my life, and my ability to keep playing guitar. Several weeks later, I moved in with my friend Marc on the west side of town, and continued to work at the children's center. I began making plans to drive my van cross country to the west coast in the near future. I told the boys in my cottage, I was moving to California in the summer.

17 - Going Out With a Bang

Summer was finally here, and I was ready to head west in my van. The day of my departure finally came, and the boys were moping around the cottage with long faces. As I was saying my goodbyes, they made a final request. The boys wanted to take turns parking my van one more time before I left. I used to let them take turns parking my van next to the cottage after returning from a field trip. I would sit on top of the engine compartment next to the driver's seat, and coach them through the exercise. It was a small thing for me to give, but they loved it. So I agreed, and the parking commenced. One by one they successfully drove up the long driveway, applied the brakes, and put it in park.

The last boy to park my van was Tony. As a recent arrival, he had never parked it before. In fact, Tony had never been behind the wheel of any motor vehicle. He was very nervous, and I assured him he would do just fine. I began coaching him through each step, with calm reassurance. Turn the key and start the engine, put your foot on the brake, move the shift lever from Park to Drive, lift your foot off the brake, place it on the gas pedal, and slowly push down to move the vehicle forward.

For the next few seconds, things seemed to be happening in slow motion. Tony froze with his right foot pressed hard on the gas, and I attempted to get my left foot on the brake. Suddenly there was a very loud crash, and the van was wrapped around a tree at the end of the driveway. Tony began screaming hysterically that he was sorry for wrecking my van. I assured him it was no big deal, and the only important thing was that we were not seriously injured. I venture to say that every employee and resident soon arrived on the scene to get a firsthand look.

Several senior staff members inspected Tony, and he appeared to be completely unharmed. The van had struck the tree dead on, leaving the driver and passenger areas fairly intact. The center of the front end was another story. That's where I was, sitting on the engine compartment. The tree was lodged against the front of the engine compartment where my right leg was at the time of impact. My left leg was near the brake pedal, and had escaped injury.

I was very grateful that Tony was unharmed. After calming down, he came over to apologize again for ruining my van, with tears streaming down his face. I did my very best to convince him I didn't care about the van, and was only concerned for his well-being. The paramedics soon arrived, and began examining me. They determined that I was in shock, placed an oxygen mask on my face, and a blanket on my body. It took the infamous

Jaws of Life to free my leg, and pull me from the wreckage.

I was taken by ambulance to the hospital and given various tests before receiving news that my leg was broken near the ankle, and my tendons had snapped as the tree forced my foot to bend upward, beyond its normal range of motion. They said I was very lucky, and it could have been much worse. My leg was put into a cast and I was released from the hospital. The van was totaled, and so were my plans.

18 - New York City Rescue

Marc's friend Dave roomed with us for a couple of months before enlisting in the Coast Guard. His nick name was Buh. I never did learn how he came by that name, but everybody used it. Buh was a likeable, easy going individual. He figured the Coast Guard was a safer bet than the army, and he wanted to get the education benefits while seeing the world outside of Syracuse.

One day, Marc received a phone call from Buh's mother. Dave had been admitted to a mental ward in a hospital on Staten Island. He had been falsely accused of murder, and after many hours of intense interrogation, confessed to a crime he never committed. They pushed him so hard and so long, he just snapped. Weeks later, the truth was uncovered and the real criminal was arrested. It turns out that another Coast Guard sailor with the exact full name had committed the crime. That man was convicted and sentenced. Buh was given an apology, and released from custody but the damage was done. He was in a catatonic state, unable to function normally.

Buh's mother was hoping we could visit her son, and trigger something to help draw him out of his condition. We were on a Greyhound bus for New York City that Friday night when Marc got home from work. We arrived very late that night, and found ourselves wandering down Second Avenue until the break of day. It was a long night of endless proposals from the ladies who worked that stretch. The later it got, the older they got. The approach was almost always identical. They would step out from the shadows, open their coat and say "Going down tonight honey?" Our reply was always the same. "No thank you, not tonight."

Morning finally broke and we were ready for breakfast. We stepped inside a busy diner, sat down at the counter, and proceeded to wait. About ten minutes had passed when we heard a loud voice from the kitchen say "Speak up boys! What do you want?" We were not in Syracuse anymore. Marc and I called out our order and the food landed in front of us in a matter of minutes. After a solid meal, we ventured off to the Staten Island Ferry by subway.

We arrived to find Buh wandering the halls in his hospital gown. He barley recognized us, and spoke with a low mumbling voice. We tried to spark some life in him by kidding around like the old days, but it wasn't working. It was time for a new plan. We stepped aside, and asked God for help. The idea came to mind that we should get Buh out of that place for a field trip.

The staff was not agreeable at first, but we

persisted. We had to convince them we were not going to get Buh high on drugs or alcohol, and that we would bring him back in time for dinner. They agreed, and we convinced Buh to change his clothes. Jeans, T shirt, tennis shoes, ball cap, and we were ready to roll.

Little by little, Buh began to emerge from his shell that day. He was able to share what he had been through, and we encouraged him to move on with his life. We rented bicycles in Central Park, and ate hot dogs from a street vendor. By the time we returned Buh to that hospital, the staff could not believe it was the same person. He thanked us profusely, and promised to get back home as soon as possible.

Buh was able to reduce his medications over the next few months, and they released him to go home. When we reunited in Syracuse, he presented Marc and me with an original painting he had done in our honor. It depicts an eagle, rescuing a small bird and carrying it to safety. He said the eagle represented

Marc and myself, and he was the small helpless bird. He said we saved his life that day in New York City.

19 - California Dreaming Becomes a Reality

Soon after that, Marc and I moved in with our friend Werner on the north side of town. Without an income, I was losing what little I had saved, quickly. I couldn't afford a vehicle, I couldn't afford rent, and I couldn't afford a plane ticket to California. I needed a job, and I needed it fast. I began searching for work on a daily basis. Back then you read about jobs in the newspaper, or heard about them through the grape vine. And just as true today, it was who you knew that really mattered. One evening, Werner was driving me home after a job interview. I thought something was odd when we parked the car in front of the apartment. There were more cars on the street than usual. I had no idea what was going on as we approached the door.

I stepped inside, the lights went on, and a large group of friends yelled "Surprise!" A banner on the wall read something like "Have a Great Time in California!" I was presented with an envelope, and inside was a farewell card signed by practically everyone I knew. Also inside, was a one way plane ticket to California. Marc had taken up a collection, and everyone who signed that card contributed to the cause. In a matter of days, I landed at LAX and was headed south to Orange County, California.

Rick and I soon rented our own place in Santa Ana. It was a new complex on the outskirts of town, called the Californian Apartments. It was near the freeway, and there was a bus stop right at the corner for me. I found a job in Costa Mesa working at a small factory in the machine shop. Initially, I did simple repetitive tasks like drilling holes with a jig and a drill press. But as fate would have it, my boss was starting to flake out and miss work a lot. John, the plant manager, took me under his wing and began training me to take his place. Before long, I was managing the machine shop and supervising a small crew.

Rick worked as a sports car mechanic for a place that sold used Ferraris. One of his coworkers owned a 1957 Peugeot that needed work, and was willing to let me use the car if I could get it running. Rick and I spent nights and weekends tearing down the engine and getting that car ready to roll. We did most of the work ourselves, with the exception of having the engine block machined. It took a couple of months to finish the work and put it all back together, but the day finally arrived.

I'll never forget the feeling when that engine fired up on the first try. Rick and I took that baby for a test ride down Newport Boulevard and onto the freeway, laughing all the way. No more standing on corners, waiting for the bus. No more long bus rides to and from work. No more asking friends to drive me here and there. And most important of all, now I could take a girl out on a date.

Rick and I were deathly afraid of the ocean when we first arrived in California, having only swam in lakes before. We decided to overcome our fears by taking a hands on aquatics training course. A successful candidate could be certified in scuba, senior life saving, senior first aid, and water safety instructor. We had no idea what was in store when we showed up that first evening. The instructor was a former Navy Seal named Steve. He and his assistant Scott would conduct the training exercises and certification exams.

There must have been about seventy applicants sitting in the class room that first night. Steve made it clear from the beginning that his program was not for someone looking to have a good time and enhance their social life. This was for those who wanted to become professional life guards, scuba instructors, or commercial divers. To weed out casual attendees, the remainder of the evening was spent in the water. We were instructed to suit up and jump into an Olympic size pool just outside.

You were to remain in the water without touching the bottom or the sides, until your name was called. When called, you were to swim twenty complete laps in a designated period of time. Only after completing the twenty laps, were you allowed to exit the water. The time was approximately six thirty pm, and the exercise would conclude at ten. Tread water for three hours without touching the bottom or side of the pool.

To many, that seemed like an impossible task. The class was diminishing in number quite rapidly. Rick and I made a pact. We would have to be pulled out of the water unconscious, before giving up. Very soon, that scenario seemed likely for both of us. Steve's assistant Scott swam up to us with one question. "How bad do you want this?" We replied "Really bad." Scott made an offer we couldn't refuse. If we would listen to every word and follow every instruction, he would coach us through the ordeal. We agreed, and swim school was in session.

He taught us to mix it up while staying afloat. Dead man's float, back float, traditional water treading etc. Then he coached us on how to get our twenty laps in under the time limit. At the end of the night, we were both admitted into the program along with about twenty others. That was just the beginning. We trained in the class room, the pool, and the ocean for the next ten weeks. It was a rigorous program to put it mildly.

The course included things like rough water rescue, and CPR. We weren't trained on plastic dummies. We had to perform CPR on each other. And if it wasn't done right, the stomach would inflate instead of the lungs. You did it over and over, until you got it right. One of the most intense exercises was to perform CPR as you rescued a swimmer from rough waters through the heavy surf. There was no faking it, because a monitor was with you all the way to shore. If it wasn't done to his satisfaction, you did it again.

Other exercises included things like finding your

way to shore underwater, at night, without a mask. You had to feel the bottom of the ocean with your hand, to determine where the shoreline would be. When all was said and done, we were fully certified and no longer afraid of the ocean. We did however, develop a healthy respect for it.

I found part time work as a pool lifeguard and enrolled as a music student at Golden West College. I played clarinet in the orchestra, studied music theory, worked part time in the school theatre, studied electronics, and took part in the inaugural Recording Arts program. Then something happened, and my immediate plans for the future changed.

20 - Love Is In The Air

Before Rick's girlfriend moved to California, her parents Don and Jeannine hosted a bible study on Wednesday nights. Werner, Rick, and myself, attended those meetings on a regular basis. After moving to California, Jeannine met some people who knew a travelling preacher named Harry. He was a likeable old fellow, with a certain charm about him. He travelled from coast to coast, meeting in homes with people he had connected with over the years.

As it happened one Saturday night, Harry was meeting with a group of believers at a large historic home in San Clemente, named Casa Romantica. The name means Romantic House, and it definitely lived up to its name that night. That's where I met my wife Susan, thirty seven years ago. I saw her from across the massive living room, with her long blond hair, wearing farmer style overalls and a plaid shirt. Her smile said everything I needed to know, and I have never seen a more beautiful woman to this day.

I was standing near the kitchen, and noticed a young mom getting water for her baby. I asked if she knew the blond girl in the overalls, and she said "That's my sister." Of course the next question was in regards to her relationship status. I was elated to learn that Susan was not currently involved in a romantic relationship. As the evening was coming to a close, I began to panic. How do I get connected with Susan? That's when a divine appointment took place right before my eyes. Susan's brother Richard was making plans with my friend Rick to go scuba diving the next day.

I introduced myself to Richard, and asked if I could join them on the dive. He said it was an excellent idea because his sister Susan needed a dive partner. I thought "This is too good to be true. I must be dreaming!" Without being on an official date, I spent my first hours with Susan underwater, as her dive partner. When the dive was over, we spent the afternoon at Susan and Richard's ocean front home in Laguna Beach. I was thinking "You're in over your head. This girl is way out of your league."

It turned out that Susan's parents were not members of the wealthy elite or anything like that. They were hard working people who had been blessed by God. They were a down to earth family, who happened to live on the beach. I began dating Susan, and a year later we became husband and wife. Our first home was in Huntington Beach, at the Apple Apartments. Susan was still in school at Long Beach State, and I had taken a job as an electronics technician.

My whole life had been leading up to this. I was ready to live happily ever after with my beautiful California girl. What more could a boy from Syracuse, New York possibly need.

21 - Trouble in Paradise

I didn't know it then, but I had placed Susan on a very high pedestal, expecting her to be my savior. Years later I came to realize, only God can fill that role in a person's life. I believed those love songs, and convinced myself she was all I needed to be happy for the rest of my days. When the honeymoon was over, and the reality of day to day life set in, I became depressed. I asked Susan for a few days alone to sort things out, and she left to stay with her parents.

About a week later, I came to grips with myself and asked her to come back home. Thankfully, she came back and we began our journey together. We had each other, and we had friends, but something was missing. Susan finally graduated Long Beach State and began working as a pediatric physical therapist.

After a series of unfortunate events, my company shut down and I was forced to change jobs. I went to work for a company that made electronic voting equipment. I hired on as an electronics technician, and soon became manager of the test department. Before we knew it, Susan was pregnant with our first child.

During an election season, we were hitting the road to support our customers in places like Texas, North Carolina, and Colorado. My son Robin was born, and I was leaving town on a regular basis for the first year of his life. When I was home, my priorities were focused on the job, and the after work socializing. Susan and I were slowly drifting apart, and I didn't have a clue.

Susan's sister Cheryl and her husband were living in a small rental, on her parent's ocean front property in Laguna Beach. They had been there for several years, and now had two children. They were moving to a bigger place, and we were offered the beach rental. It was a beautiful property with stunning views of the Pacific Ocean, and private access to the water. Most would describe it as paradise on earth.

What we didn't see coming, was the endless flow of friends who wanted to stop by and visit. They brought their friends, their neighbors, their relatives, their coworkers, their drugs, and their booze. Before long it became party central, and our privacy was a thing of the past. It didn't seem to matter what day or what time it was, they just showed up. They offered to share the treats, and I accepted. The party life style was taking a serious toll on our marriage.

22 - The Waterfall – Turn Around

Susan and I befriended a fun loving couple who liked to let it all hang out. George and Christy had recently completed a self-awareness program, and invited us to check it out. We were looking to expand our horizons, and this seemed like a good way to get started. At the time, we didn't attend church, and had very little contact with other Christians. Our Bibles were collecting dust.

One beautiful summer day, a few of us decided to embark on an off road wilderness adventure. George was an experienced four wheeler, and knew of a remote waterfall in the Cleveland National

Forest. We climbed into his Jeep, and headed for the hills. As a matter of routine, I smoked a little weed and downed a few beers along the way. We finally arrived at the trail head and hiked out to the top of the falls.

Tenaja Falls is a 150 foot, tiered waterfall, cascading over slippery granite. The first drop is very short, and ends in a small pool suitable for swimming. It can easily be climbed down or jumped into when the water is deep enough. This is where we planned to take a dip before heading back. Beyond the first pool, the next drop is very steep. An idea came to mind as I surveyed the area. I could lower myself down to the edge, jump horizontally across the water, and climb back up the other side. This would really impress my friends!

When I got down to the edge, I realized it was impossible. There wasn't enough room to get the running start I would need to do it. I would have to slide back up the same way I came down. There was only one problem. The rocks in this area were smooth, wet, and slippery. Going up would be much more difficult without the help of gravity or something to grab a hold of. The only other alternative was down, and this was not an option. Apart from the waterfall itself, the sides were extremely steep and covered with jagged rock. This drop was well over fifty feet down with a small, shallow pool at the bottom.

I was in big trouble, and I knew it. I began to sense a dark presence around me. At first I tried to ignore it and stay positive, but it was too strong. This was a serious situation. My friends began to yell and scream for me to stay put while they figured something out. If I slipped while attempting to slide back up, I would fall face forward onto the steep jagged rocks below. In this scenario, there was no doubt that my life would be over.

Strange things began to happen. Everything became silent around me. It was as if someone turned down the volume on a stereo or television set. I could see everything, but there was no sound.

My friends were still yelling and screaming, but I could only see their lips moving, and their hands waving. There was total silence.

I felt that my life was about to end, and I felt deep regret for letting Susan down. I had to do something. I made a decision to carefully slide back up the wet rocks. Just as I began to make a move, I heard a loud, authoritative voice, in my right ear. "Turn around!" This was not an internal voice in my mind. It was external. At this very instant I began to slip, and the command was repeated with more intensity. "Turn around!!" Instantly, I turned my whole body to the right and found myself immersed in water. I was facing the slimy rock surface behind the waterfall. The now calm voice, spoke audibly once more. "Relax, everything is alright. You're going to be just fine." I completely relaxed, and felt very peaceful.

I could feel the slimy surface with my hands and feet as I found myself sliding on all fours into the pool of water at the bottom of the drop. I stood up in knee deep water and raised my head to see where I had fallen from. It was a long way up. I had been saved from certain death, by divine intervention. I walked into the wooded area to my left and found a winding trail that leads all the way back to the top.

Susan was angry with me for carelessly getting into a life and death situation. She was convinced that I was going to die or become severely disabled. My friends thought I had just pulled off a daring stunt. I was just happy to be alive and completely unharmed.

I would love to say this miracle turned my life around and brought me back to God. It was almost the opposite. I was feeling invincible with a new lease on life. I was ready to do whatever I thought would make me happy. I did nothing to deserve God's mercy that day, and without his intervention, I would have been dashed to pieces on the rocks. In retrospect, it's hard to believe I didn't see it as a wakeup call.

The days and months rolled by, and I continued on my self-destructive path. One Friday afternoon, I borrowed my father in law's pickup and drove to Newport Beach. An old acquaintance from Syracuse, had just opened a hot dog shop near the ocean. He wasn't licensed to sell beer, so I grabbed a six pack and hit the road. I thought it was pretty clever disguising my beer with replica soda can wraps. As evening turned to night I headed for home.

I had never used the pickup at night before, and wasn't familiar with the headlight switch. I was pulled over for driving at night with only my parking lights on. No amount of charm and smooth talk could change the officer's mind. I was arrested for driving under the influence and taken to jail. Susan bailed me out at four in the morning and I was feeling pretty ashamed of myself. This was another call to turn my life around, and once again, I missed it.

23 - Rock and Roll

As a massage therapist, my brother in law landed a few clients in the entertainment business. Eventually this led to a position with the local concert production company. Joe enlisted friends and family members to work behind the scenes at various concert venues in the area. Essentially, we fulfilled back stage contract requirements for each performing act. This mostly consisted of food and beverages to be delivered at specific times, in a specific manner. The work was hard, the hours were long, and the party continued after the show was over

I was already living the lifestyle, so this was a natural fit for me. I continued to write music, and managed to record a few demos. Susan and I would drive up to Hollywood and present my songs to producers and publishers at songwriter showcase events almost every week. I even landed a couple of performances at the world famous Troubadour, but nothing ever came of it.

My job ended when the company went bankrupt and sold to a competitor. I signed a consulting contract with the new owners, and was employed for several months with a pretty decent salary. After that, I started my own consulting business with former clients whose systems were no longer under warranty. The money was good, and the freedom was even better. This allowed me to continue working back stage at concerts, writing new songs, and living the rock and roll life.

Susan wanted another baby, and before long our daughter Lauren was born. On the surface, things seemed to be okay. In reality, Susan and I were both looking for something to fill the emptiness in our lives. I was away a lot, and wasn't really there when I came back. Susan began to look elsewhere for relational intimacy, and I continued to indulge in my addictions. We both had unresolved issues from our childhood, and they were beginning to play out in our adult lives. In less than ten years of marriage, we had become totally disconnected from each other.

By the time I realized what was going on, our marriage was just about over. Susan asked me to move out and suggested I get counseling to help me deal with the divorce. It was one of the worst feelings I have ever experienced. I asked myself "How did I screw up the best thing that ever happened to me?" Then I got down on my knees and begged God to give me another chance with Susan. I asked him to restore my broken marriage.

24 - The Bridge – It's Right In Front of You

Susan and I began counseling with separate therapists to help us deal with the impending divorce. Individually, we discovered that our own issues overshadowed the issues with our marriage. Within minutes of starting the first session, I broke down in tears as I recalled my troubled past. Over the next few weeks, Susan's therapist convinced her to put the divorce on hold while she dealt with her own issues. The only thing certain for either one of us, was the need for healing and change.

Eventually, both therapists recommended joint counseling to work on our marriage. We did just that, and when all was said and done, there was a small ray of hope. It was going to take some time and effort, but for the moment, Susan agreed to give it another try. I was ready to step away from the concert scene, and we were both ready to get away from the beach party. Life at the beach just seemed to attract some pretty unhealthy elements.

My idea of getting away was different from Susan's. I wanted to pick up and move the whole family to Syracuse, New York. Susan just wanted a little distance from her parents and the beach party. She reluctantly agreed to my plan under a set of conditions. Go ahead to Syracuse, get a job, rent a house, move our belongings in, and then she would consider the move. I called my friend Marc, bought him a one way ticket to California, packed up our belongings, and stuffed them into a U-Haul trailer.

As we were getting ready to roll, I grabbed a few tools from the trunk of my car. One tool in particular, kept catching my eye. It was a large adjustable wrench, made of heavy steel. It had a long handle, and looked like something you might see in a museum. It weighed a lot too. It originally belonged to Susan's grandfather. I tried hard to ignore it, but something or someone, kept telling me to bring that wrench. I finally gave in and placed it in the bed of my little Isuzu pickup truck.

Marc and I hit the road and made our way across the country with only one near catastrophe. We were somewhere in the Midwest, travelling at a good clip on the interstate, when we noticed something strange up ahead. It was a bouncing, spinning, metal object. It appeared to get larger and faster as it approached our vehicle head on. We were mesmerized, as it took a final bounce straight for our windshield. Suddenly, it glanced off the hood and bounced clear over the top of my truck.

After letting out a collective "Yipes!" we named the object Death Ball 5000. Soon after, we passed a pickup truck full of used auto parts. Our best guess was that a U-Joint had bounced out and on to the pavement. We finally stopped for gas and examined the hood of my truck. We were saved, with less than an inch to spare.

The move to Syracuse was short lived. A few months after my arrival, I decided to head back. The job market was dismal, and I really missed Susan and the kids. I love Syracuse, and I truly enjoy our visits there with family and friends. But Susan and the kids were my home now, and that's where I needed to be. I rented another U-Haul trailer and Marc graciously helped pack it all up again. I said my goodbyes and hit the road for a solo cross country trip to Laguna Beach, California.

My plan was to drive about seven or eight hours a day and spend the night at inexpensive motels along the way. Day three arrived and I was ready to roll with enthusiasm. Today I would head through Memphis, cross the Mississippi River into Arkansas and spend the night in Oklahoma City. The sun was shining and the sky was clear. Things were going smooth until I was making my way up the Mississippi River Bridge on Interstate 40. There are three lanes, and I was in the middle with a full load of cars and trucks around me. Suddenly, people were honking horns and flashing lights to get my attention. The U-Haul trailer had come unhitched from my truck. Looking in the rear view mirror, I could see the trailer swerving from side to side behind me. The only thing keeping it connected to my truck were two small safety chains.

I have no idea how I managed to get that trailer and my truck through heavy traffic over to the side of the bridge. I just turned my wheel to the right and started praying. Before I knew it, there I was. A quick assessment revealed the problem. The nut which holds the ball in place, had come loose and was now missing. Examining the threaded bolt, I could see this was a serious piece of hardware. Much larger than anything I might find in my tool box. The wires connecting the truck lights to the trailer lights were also broken. That I could fix with wire strippers and electrical tape which I had with me. Before long, everything was back in place except the missing nut.

I searched through my supply of miscellaneous hardware to no avail. Then I conducted a thorough search of the narrow shoulders on both sides of the bridge. I walked up one side and then down the other. Within an hour or two, I had a pretty impressive collection of nuts. I was certain one of them would fit, and have just the right thread to match. I got down on my back and tried every single one. They were either too small, too big, or not the right thread. Now what do I do? The day was slipping by fast. I tried flagging down a ride back into Memphis, but the bridge is not an easy place to stop and pick up passengers, let alone a total stranger.

I started to pray, "Lord, where can I get the part I need?" The answer came quickly and clearly. "It's right in front of you." I asked, "Lord, is that really you or am I just saying what I want to hear?" The answer was the same. "It's right in front of you." I began to think outside the box and came up with an idea. I thought, "Maybe there's another part of my truck, or this trailer, I can borrow just to get me by until the next town." I started searching under the hood and anywhere else I could, for a nut to remove.

There was nothing even close to what I needed. The sun was getting ready to set, and I did not want to spend the night on that bridge. Once it became dark, the risk of someone hitting me would increase significantly. I began to pray with more intensity than before. "Lord, what should I do?" The answer came back the same. "It's right in front of you." Now I was getting angry. God is telling me something I just don't understand, or I'm going nuts. No pun intended.

I began to challenge The Lord. "Okay Lord, if it's right in front of me, I'll just put out my hand and touch it!" Almost mockingly, with eyes closed, I reached out and placed my hand on something right in front of me. When I opened my eyes, I was looking at one of the nuts used to attach a metal railing to the bridge. They were in groups of four, at an interval of about every ten feet or so.

I thought to myself, "Could this be just the right size and thread I need? Even if it is, how in the world could I manage to remove one of these things? I'm sure they are on plenty tight and haven't budged in many years." Just then, I flashed back to Grandpa's solid steel, oversized pipe wrench. I remembered that distinct voice, telling me to bring it along. Without further hesitation, I grabbed the wrench and secured it to one of the nuts. It took a lot of leverage, using my legs and feet, to break the nut loose. It finally came free and I was holding it in my hand. I looked up and said "Lord, if this thing fits, I will never doubt you again."

I got down on my back, took a long pause, and placed the nut over the bolt. It fit perfectly! I threaded that nut on the bolt and tightened it good and secure with Grandpa's wrench! As the sun was beginning to set in front of me, I drove over that bridge praising The Lord at the top of my lungs for miles to come! God never lies. It was just as he said it was, right in front of me.

25 - Proud New Home Owners

Crossing that bridge and arriving safe in California, was just the beginning. I was glad to be home, but our marriage had a long way to go on the road to recovery and restoration.

We began looking to rent somewhere close to, but not on the beach. During our weeks of searching, a friend let us spend weekends at his rustic cabin in the desert. We really enjoyed those times as a family. We went on hikes together, and spent evenings around the camp fire. Robin and I brought along our radio controlled, off road racing cars, and let them fly through the desert terrain.

Before long, we found a place that seemed just right for us. It was in a family friendly neighborhood, at the end of a cull de sac. It was also one block from a bike path leading to the beach. We met the owners, filled out the application, and said a prayer. Al and Anita said we reminded them of younger days, when they were starting out. Within a few hours, they called to give us the good news. We were moving to San Juan Capistrano!

One of the first things we noticed was that our list of friends got instantly smaller. People were not stopping by at all hours anymore. In fact, most of them were not stopping by at all. Life got simpler. We spent time riding our bikes to the beach, swimming at the community pool, playing in the park and growing vegetables in our garden. Robin and Lauren were busy playing with new friends in the neighborhood. This was a big change from Laguna, where there were no kids to play with. For a few years, life seemed to get better.

Then one day, a real estate agent came by. She

asked a few questions, and we were off to look at homes. The idea of owning our own place felt pretty good. We settled on a price range and began our search. We had no idea what to expect for less than two hundred thousand dollars in 1991. I wasn't impressed with our initial viewings and then came the condo on Leo Lane. Two stories, three bedrooms, and a small enclosed patio backing up to a spacious greenbelt.

The price was right and the deal was done in a matter of weeks. We were proud new home owners in Lake Forest, CA.

26 - Haunted House

The spiritual realm is a strange concept for most people. Until I experienced a few miracles, I wasn't really sure what to think about it myself. Jesus healed my hand overnight, saved my life several times, and gave me a second chance with Susan just to name a few. But up to this point, I had only noticed good things happening in the spiritual realm. That was about to change.

It started with the kids, and then Susan. They began telling me about strange noises in the house. My daughter heard a ball bouncing on the ceiling above her bed. My son heard children running up and down the stairs. Susan heard cabinet drawers opening and closing. Most of this was happening at night. For whatever reason, I was in denial or I just didn't hear what they were hearing.

When we bought the condo, our plan was to stay for about five years and then move up to a detached house. The economy and real estate market had other plans. Five years came and went, with no light at the end of the tunnel. We decided to fix the place up and settle in for the long haul. We did just that, and the strange noises continued. I really thought they were imagining things. Eventually, while in the house alone for a few days, I heard everything. Those strange noises were very real.

Then something changed all our lives. Lauren was about twelve, when a school nurse noticed something different about her back. She recommended seeing an orthopedic surgeon for further evaluation. Lauren was diagnosed with Kyphosis. A spinal disorder which can lead to severe curvature of the back if untreated. There were only two options for treatment.

One option was to have a metal rod surgically fused to Lauren's spine. She would not be able to bend above her hips at all. The second option was to wear a body brace from her neck down to her hips, twenty four hours a day. She could only remove it to bathe, once a day. There would be no bending with this option either. Lauren was just beginning to blossom as a beautiful young girl. She played violin in the school band, and was learning to swing dance. Her new social life was immediately put on hold.

We opted for the brace, and enrolled Lauren in a computer based home school. In miraculous timing, I was presented with an opportunity to work from home. Lauren had always been a good student, and this seemed like a reasonable solution. I got busy with the job in my new office upstairs, and Lauren studied on the computer downstairs. Like those strange noises in the house, I also failed to notice what was happening to my daughter. She began withdrawing into a dark, depressing world.

27 - A Dark Holiday Season

Lauren began to meet people on the internet, and formed a new social network of friends. She was writing poetry, and drawing. She even had a web site to share her work. As parents, we were not allowed to see any of Lauren's poetry or drawings. She insisted on having a private place to share with her friends. Sometime after that, Lauren began cutting herself. It took a while to discover, because she hid the cuts beneath her clothing.

Suicide attempts, and boys from out of state soon followed. Weekly sessions with psychologists and counselors, a Bi-Polar diagnosis, and various mood altering prescription drugs came after that. Lauren was getting frustrated, and so were we. Susan and I began hanging out at the new brew pub in town, and unknown to us, Lauren began using drugs.

Lauren's counselor called her on the drug use, and she profusely denied it. She agreed to a drug test, and a family counseling session. Over lunch the day before our family session, Lauren assured me her counselor was wrong about the drug use.

The holiday season was just around the corner. I love this time of year. At my old job, they called me Father Christmas. The morning came, and we prepared to meet with Lauren's counselor. There was only one problem. Lauren was nowhere to be found. We called every possible friend we could think of, and then some.

I hacked into Lauren's email account, found more names and numbers, and discovered she was in fact using drugs. I also found the web address for Lauren's poetry and art site. This is where we learned the severity of her depression. Most of her poetry and drawings depicted blood and death. We contacted the authorities and reported Lauren as a missing person. Surprisingly, there wasn't much they could do. They interviewed us, interviewed her friends, and followed up on a few leads. As it turned out, California law wouldn't allow them to bring Lauren home even if they located her. The law protects a minor from being returned to a potentially abusive situation at home.

Days went by, and still no word. Then we received a message from one of Lauren's friends. Tell my mom and dad not to worry. She had run away on her own, and was fine. We were obligated to inform the authorities, and Lauren was no longer considered a missing person.

Thanksgiving Day arrived, and Lauren called briefly to tell us she was sorry, and that she loved us. Christmas came and went, and so did New Year's Day. It was a dark holiday season. We began to wonder if we would ever see our daughter again.

28 - Tough Love and Hard Choices

Lauren's counselor wasn't surprised to learn of her disappearance. She called a family session to discuss the situation. Susan, myself, and our son Robin sat down and listened with one common purpose. We would do whatever we could, to save Lauren. I now believe only God can do this if we are ready for help, and ultimately, the choice is ours.

We were given an option to explore, and advised to use it if Lauren ever came home. Susan and I spent the next few weeks researching out of state rehab programs. We knew Lauren would never agree to this voluntarily. In order for something like this to work, all arrangements would have to be made in advance. If she came home, we would place one phone call to set things in motion. After that, a team of professionals would escort Lauren from our home to a rehab facility in St. George, Utah.

This was by far, the hardest decision we have ever made. We did everything in our power to insure they were a reputable organization, and they would not harm Lauren. Susan and I, along with our son Robin, talked, and prayed about this decision for days. We all agreed on one thing. We loved Lauren enough to give it a chance, if she ever came home again.

Several months later, that day arrived. Lauren wasn't home for more than a few hours, when she started talking about leaving again. We made the call, and in the middle of the night, they came and took her away. The three of us stayed up all night waiting for word that she had safely arrived in St.

George. The call came almost nine hours later. Lauren had arrived safe and sound.

The program usually began with a wilderness camping experience, but Lauren needed time to get healthy and come down from the drugs. They assured us she would never be physically or mentally abused at any time during her stay. Just knowing she was off the drugs was enough to help us sleep better. A few weeks later, she made it through the wilderness experience, and was now attending high school classes.

Part of the program required parents to come and participate in weekend seminars. Several months later, Susan and I were headed to St. George for our first visit and seminar with Lauren. To say this was an emotional experience, would be an understatement. I can't begin to explain just how emotional it was to see Lauren for the first time since watching her being driven away by total strangers. Our time together was brief and very structured. We talked, and cried, and laughed. We participated in group therapy sessions, and all too soon said our tearful goodbyes.

For the next eight months, things were looking up. We felt good about the program, and Lauren was looking healthier than ever. We participated in more seminars, and she was finally caught up in school. Her senior year was approaching, and Susan wanted Lauren to graduate from high school back home. I missed Lauren as much as Susan did, and against all professional advice, we brought her home. There is no one to blame for what happened next, except the devil himself. Within weeks, Lauren picked up where she had left off nine months earlier.

29 - Divine Appointments

During those years, I had several encounters with individuals who seemed to know what was going on in my life without being told. This typically happened while travelling, and usually in an airport. On one such occasion, I sat next to a man in silence while drinking my beer. With no invitation or so much as a glance, he started speaking to me. The first words out of his mouth were "I know what you're going through. I've been there."

I politely said he had no idea what I was going through, since we had never met or spoken before. Unfazed by my response, he proceeded. "She started cutting, then the suicide attempts and trips to the mental clinic. My wife was losing her mind. I thought she was going to end up in a mental ward. Hang in there my friend, there's hope. My daughter finally came out okay." I was speechless. Then before I could finish my beer and pay the tab he was gone.

Susan and I had an encounter while taking a walk on one of our camping trips. We had stayed at this location before, but never ventured out of the campground. Walking along a country road, we noticed some model homes on top of a steep hill. Susan suggested we go up and have a look. My only thought was "Who would buy a house out here?"

We made our way up the hill, only to learn the models were not open for viewing yet. We would have to come back a little later to see the homes. Down the hill we went. Then Susan mentioned seeing an Open House sign just past the model homes. She wanted to walk up the hill again and have a look. Up we went, for the second time.

Walking in the front door we were greeted by a pleasant young woman. She had blonde hair, and couldn't have been much more than thirty. We exchanged a little small talk while she gave us a tour of the downstairs. She encouraged us to have a look upstairs and to let her know if we had any questions. As we made our way out of the master bedroom, she met us in the hallway. "You guys aren't interested in buying a house are you?"

Within a few more seconds of conversation, we began talking about our struggles with Lauren. She was ecstatic. She couldn't wait to tell us about her morning. For starters, she arrived an hour earlier than usual. She observed us walking up the hill, both times. She couldn't help but wonder where we had come from and why we didn't have a car. She just couldn't stop thinking about us. She said "Now I know why you're here. I'm a prayer warrior, and we are here to pray for your daughter." We all held hands and had a very intense prayer session right there. She also had some encouraging words for us.

30 - An Answer to Prayer

It was now 2007. Eight years had gone by since Lauren put on that body brace. Her physical health and emotional state were not good. In August, Susan's father had a stroke. We were on our summer vacation when it happened, and spent the next three days making trips between the hospital and the beach. He died on the third day, and we headed for home. Our next door neighbor said she could hear Lauren crying. She was grieving the loss or her grandpa.

Thanksgiving came, and Susan's mom was doing her best to carry on without Bob. Sarah was very concerned about Lauren. As Christmas approached, she developed a sizable open wound on her leg. She was in need of immediate medical attention. Sarah offered to drive Lauren to a doctor, but she would have nothing to do with it. Fortunately, she sought treatment at an urgent care center the next day. She had developed a staph infection. To put it mildly, Lauren was a wreck.

Two weeks before Christmas, Susan and I were attending her annual company party. We were compelled to seek out believers, and ask them to pray for Lauren. Total desperation had set in, and we were asking for a miracle. The answer came on December 15th as we were celebrating Robin's 26th birthday. Lauren was late for the party, but that wasn't unusual. I have a history of running late for everything.

Susan's cell phone rang, and it was Lauren. "Where are you Lauren?" A slight pause, "I'm in jail mom. I've been arrested." I can still hear grandma's reaction to this day. "Praise the Lord!"

This was the answer to all of our prayers. For the next two days, Lauren begged and yelled at us to bail her out. It was difficult to say no, but we held our ground.

She spent the next six months, confined to a small cell for twenty two hours a day. We would visit every Friday, from behind a small glass window. On our first visit, we told Lauren she would have to live somewhere else when she was released. The impact was visible on Lauren's face. We loved our daughter very much, but could no longer tolerate the chaos and turmoil her lifestyle brought into our home.

A friend in the legal system referred us to a good lawyer. Lauren would be paying the bill with an inheritance from her grandparents. It felt like we had come to the end of a long downward journey, and were about to begin a new chapter.

31 - A Pause to Reflect

Pausing here to reflect, there was a lot going on in parallel during those years. In 2000, we finally sold the condo and found a house in Rancho Santa Margarita. There was a short window of opportunity before home prices would raise beyond our reach. We qualified for a loan and began a sixty day escrow. As the closing date approached, our realtor became concerned. She was unable to contact the buyer, and his agent was out of the country.

The day of closing came and went without a word from either one. Our realtor called and told me the deal was essentially dead. Even if they showed up, the seller would have to agree with an extended escrow, and we would have to submit a new loan application. The market value of that home had already increased by twenty thousand dollars. Without a miracle, the seller would never agree. When Robin came home from school, I met him at the door and asked him to pray with me. Against his agent's advice, the seller agreed, and we got the house in Rancho Santa Margarita.

Robin played little league baseball and then switched to hockey as he entered middle school. He was a goalie on both roller and ice hockey teams. He was very good, and loved the game. Eventually he played on travel teams, and we got to hang out with other players and their dads on the road. We always had fun together on those trips.

While attending college, Robin had a narrow escape. He was living in a rental owned by the parents of a classmate, and the house was being renovated to sell. Rent was reasonable, but the home's condition was a bit sketchy. On one particular day, Robin was the only one home. He was used to hearing the sounds of construction, and never gave it a second thought.

It was mid-morning when he began to feel very tired. He was just about to lay down for a nap, when he heard a strange commotion outside. As he poked his head out the front door to investigate, the workers yelled at him to get out of the house. They were unaware that someone was home, when they accidently broke a gas line. The leaking gas was causing Robin to feel sleepy.

After vacating the house, he began to feel normal. The gas company supervisor told Robin he was lucky to be alive. A lot of gas had leaked before they realized something was wrong. The broken line was directly under the house. They were attempting to level the structure with jacks, when it broke. He could have easily died in his sleep, or triggered a deadly explosion by turning on a light or a fan.

Also during this period, Susan and I returned to

our faith in God. Susan began attending Saddleback Church on a regular basis, and eventually I followed suit. We both started reading our bibles again and connecting with other believers. We were brought to our knees by the difficulties in our life. Susan also attended weekly meetings in the Celebrate Recovery program at Saddleback. She completed a twelve step course for codependency and became a leader in the program. She witnessed lives being changed, and cultivated friendships that are still going strong to this day.

Together with our friend Steve, we began to lead weekly mountain bike rides as part of Saddleback's sports ministry. I also started playing my guitar and writing songs again. Just three days after Lauren's arrest, God gave me a song to encourage our family. The opening lines go like this. "Even though we may not understand everything that's happening right now, rest assured your Father has a plan. In the end he'll work it out somehow. In our darkest hour when we're all alone, all we need to do is take his hand." The song is called Unfailing Love. I was able to play a recorded version for Lauren over the phone a few weeks later.

32 - Calming the Storm and Second Chances

Susan was prompted to buy a book and have it sent directly to Lauren in jail. She prayed for guidance in selecting something that would touch Lauren's heart. The book was "90 Minutes in Heaven" by Don Piper. She later told us it helped to read about someone in a situation worse than hers. Don was in physical pain, as well as being confined in a broken body. Lauren was confined in a tiny cell, but she was in a better place than Don had been. The next book Susan bought for Lauren was a bible.

Lauren's legal situation was serious. She and her two codefendants were facing several felony charges. Two of those charges qualified for California's three strikes law. They didn't harm anyone, but drugs, stolen property, and a gun were involved. Lauren had unknowingly driven the getaway car. To complicate the situation, all three lawyers had to agree on any arrangements made with the DA. From the beginning, we were told they were facing time in state prison.

About four months into her incarceration, we came to visit on a Friday as usual. As we sat behind the glass window, we could see Lauren approaching. There was something different about her facial expression and the way she walked. Susan and I looked at each other for a second as she sat down behind the glass. She said "Mom and dad, everything is going to be okay. Jesus is real. I've been praying and he has been answering my prayers. I asked him into my life and he told me everything is going to be okay." With each visit, we could see a difference in Lauren. She was calm and peaceful. She told us about her prayers, how God answered them, and that she was reading the bible.

She was also attending a weekly church service in jail. We thank God for this miracle almost every day.

Court dates came and went while we continued to visit Lauren and pray for her future. Months went by and her case was finally near a deadline for plea bargain. Lauren's attorney had been working with the DA to arrange for residential drug rehab, in lieu of state prison for Lauren. She was feeling confident as we entered court on the day of decision. That confidence was soon replaced with shock and disbelief, as she informed us there was no deal on the table. The DA told Lauren's attorney she had no record or memory of any communication about a drug rehab arrangement. We were told that Lauren was headed for prison.

As we began to break down, I recalled reading the bible that morning. Jesus was sleeping in the boat while a storm raged on the water. His disciples were terrified. When they woke him up, he stood and calmed the storm with a word. Susan and I prayed a desperate prayer as we sat watching tense expressions on the faces of all three lawyers and the DA. Then something strange happened. Suddenly they were all smiling, and acting cheerfully towards each other. I was perplexed to say the least.

Lauren's attorney came out from the bench to where we sat. She had a genuine look of astonishment as she said these words. "I don't know what just happened. I have never seen anything like this before. The DA suddenly changed her mind. Only one of the three is going to prison, and his attorney agreed to let Lauren and the other defendant go to rehab." Susan and I know what happened. Jesus spoke a word, and the storm was calmed.

Lauren finished her time in jail and was transferred to a residential rehab. She graduated from the program six months later, and was ready to begin a year of outpatient rehab to comply with her legal obligations. She was clearly a changed person now, and we agreed to have Lauren back home with us.

Before long, she met the love of her life. They went hiking, cooked meals together, and volunteered their time for charity. Wedding bells weren't far behind. Our son in law encouraged Lauren to seek expungement from her felony convictions, and four years after that fateful night in December, her record was expunged. God is all about second chances, and this was definitely a second chance for Lauren.

One of Lauren's best attributes is her child like faith. She trusts God for everything. She's the first one to suggest prayer, when things are going south. We are so thankful God gave us a second chance with our daughter.

A few years before, Robin met the love of his life while working in Hollywood, CA. They married, moved to the east coast, and just had a baby boy. It's hard to believe Susan and I are now grandparents. Our marriage isn't perfect, but we are deeply in love, and it's better than ever before. When asked how we stayed married for thirty seven years and still love each other, my response is always the same. "Only by the grace of God. Without him, our marriage would have been over a long time ago. I train wrecked it and Jesus put it back together."

He's in the process of putting me back together too. He continues to reveal my broken areas, and even shows me how they were broken in the first place. He promises to restore me in those places. When my heart is ready, I ask him to go ahead and do it. He's in the business of restoring things.

33 - Alive and Well

I referred to my first miracle in the opening line of this book. I also mentioned there having been many since. It's true, and they are still happening today. Some might be considered bigger than others, but they all involve someone who loves me. Not a faceless ball of energy, or light, or a cosmic force. They involve a loving father and his children. One who cares about everything. One who is very much alive and well. Having said that, here are some of the miracles I have recently experienced.

He's Got My Back

It was the first week of May 2013, and my back had

been feeling a little sore lately. Nothing unusual, considering I had been working on my sprinkler system, been on a few bike rides, fixed the drain in my shower, and did a little extra lifting at work. I wasn't really concerned. Then one morning as I was headed to work, I began feeling something beyond the usual soreness. My right leg went completely numb below the knee, and I had shooting pains down both thighs. I immediately phoned my boss and told him I was headed for the urgent care center.

The attending PA told me these were classic signs of a "sciatic nerve episode, quite common for guys my age." She prescribed a combination of drugs and three day's rest. I felt okay and returned to work, but by the end of the day things got worse. I was practically in tears from the pain. The next morning, Susan drove me back to the urgent care center. They injected me with a strong anti-inflammatory, and said I'd be feeling much better in a couple of hours. They also took a set of X-Rays and told me to make an appointment with my primary doctor to review the results. The first available appointment with my doctor, was on the following Tuesday. Several hours later, I was no better off than I was before the injection.

By the time I saw my doctor on Tuesday, I was taking double doses of pain meds just to sleep, and barely able to sit down on any surface, including the toilet. My doctor pointed out a few interesting things on the X-Rays, including an extra vertebrae at T13, and two possible compressed discs in the Lumbar region of my spine. He then referred me to a physical medicine specialist for further evaluation. The next available appointment with the specialist was in two weeks. Meanwhile, I acquired a myriad of special cushions, and a reaching device, to accommodate my situation. They were helpful at first, but as the pain increased, they became increasingly ineffective.

My back pain ordeal began in the first week of May, and on May 30th, we finally met with the specialist. She reviewed the X-Rays and ordered an

MRI. The next available MRI appointment was on June 12th, almost two weeks from then. Over the next two weeks, my pain was getting worse on a daily basis.

Months before all this began, Susan and I had planned a trip back east to visit relatives in upstate New York. The June 20th date for our trip was approaching fast. Given my inability to sit for even a few minutes, a six hour flight from California to New York looked impossible. We prayed about this many times, and continued to receive the same answer. You are going to New York.

On June 12th, I had my first MRI. Magnetic Resonance Imaging is a test which uses a magnetic field and pulses of radio wave energy, to make pictures of things inside the body. For those who may not have had this unique experience, I'll try to describe it in simple terms.

Lying flat on your back, you're inserted head first into a narrow tube like structure. You're instructed to stay very still for the next 20 minutes, and then given a small rubber device to squeeze, if you can't take it any longer. There is no physical sensation to speak of, but it's extremely claustrophobic, very loud, and just plain spooky! All I could say to the young gal who escorted me to and from my MRI was, "I don't know how anybody could get through that without talking to God." She looked at me with a sweet smile, and said "There you go!"

The next evening, I received a message from the specialist saying the MRI results were in. They identified what she called "a rather large mass" consistent with an "extruded disc" which was now lodged in my spinal nerve canal. The mass measured approximately 23 by 11 by 12 mm, and filled the entire vertical canal, pinching off the nerves. When we spoke by phone the next morning, she said "Now we know what the problem is!" I inquired about treatment options like a Steroid Epidural or Lumbar Traction, and she said that due to the size and location of the mass, surgery would likely be the best option. She then referred me to a neurosurgeon. The next available appointment was on Wednesday, June 19th, the day before our scheduled trip to New York.

The following day, I received word that a group of believers from our church, wanted to pray over me on Sunday after service. I gladly agreed to come by for prayer. In the days leading up to now, we had been asking God to give us wisdom in regards to any decisions involving surgery. His answer was consistent. He clearly said that I was not to have surgery for this issue. He also asked me to fast for three days prior to our scheduled departure for New York. He said "Give me this for three days, and watch what I will do" and so I agreed.

Sunday came around, and Susan drove me to church for prayer. Pastor Ryan and a group of strong believers, who I know well, were ready to lay hands on me and pray. Ryan looked me straight in the eye and asked this question, "What do you want us to pray for?" I love that he asked me that question, because it reminded me of how Jesus often spoke with those he was about to heal. Jesus knew that a man was blind, or deaf, or lame, and yet he would ask, "What do you want me to do for you?" I replied to Ryan "I want prayer to be healed and travel to New York."

He led the prayer as such, and we all agreed in the mighty name of Jesus Christ, by whose stripes we are healed. For the next two days, my condition worsened. It seemed as though I had a new pain and a new physical limitation each day. We were tempted to cancel our trip. On Tuesday night, June 18th, I lost it. I began grumbling and complaining, and erupted into anger at the Lord. When I finally caught myself, I got down on my knees and asked him to forgive me. In spite of the pain, I felt peace. I told Susan about my anger episode, and we individually asked God if we were to go ahead with our trip. If we both received a yes, we were going. Susan looked at me and said, "We are going, but it's going to take a miracle."

Wednesday, June 19th arrived and there was no relief in sight. Susan drove me to Anaheim, for our meeting with the neurosurgeon. As we walked into the hospital, Susan said "I feel like Jesus is walking in with us!" A cord of three strands is not easily broken. I stood in the waiting area, afraid to sit, reading a plaque on the wall with the credentials of our neurosurgeon. He was not a young man, and it appeared that he was well experienced in his field of expertise. They called our name, and in went all three of us. After a long series of strange questions, which began to irritate me, he conducted some simple neurological tests on my legs and back. Then he showed us the images from my MRI. There were various layers from different views, and they all confirmed the presence of a "rather large" mass in my spinal nerve canal. There it was in plain sight.

He proceeded to discuss all of the possible treatments available for disc related issues. There were many, but in conclusion he said all but surgery would either be ineffective or impossible, "due to the size and location of the mass." He painted a fairly bleak picture of surgery too. He said there would likely be permanent effects, due to pressing on the nerves to avoid cutting them etc. He also mentioned that he might have to go in again at a later date if more disc material leaked out into the nerve canal.

Knowing what God had spoken to us about surgery, and having already received numerous unsolicited confirmations, the consult was pretty much over. What happened next can best be described as God's perfect timing.

Before going into the neurosurgeon's office, we set our phones to silent. Something I usually forget to undo, missing calls and messages for hours later, if not days. This text came in, just as we were getting ready to leave his office and head home.

Text message from our friend Lisa:

The Holy Spirit kept prompting my memory to recall the many Miraculous healings you have witnessed already in your life...brought me to tears. I stand in belief that this will be another testimony of the Lord moving in a miraculous way in your life....He is Lord not the pain! Undone today before the Lord....in awe of His love for you!

My text response:

Wow, your text came at the exact moment our consult meeting was coming to an end. I usually don't even hear or sense that I'm being texted when my phone is on silent, but something told me to read it before we left the office. After reading your text, I stood up and without even thinking, out of my mouth comes my testimony about Jesus and how he healed the growth in my hand when I was younger. He took hold of my two hands and thanked me for sharing it with him. Of course, the "worldly" option is surgery, and he advised against a trip to NY. I'm thinking the best option is to trust God for healing and go to NY. The world view would be that I'm delusional. We've heard that one before. Then what? Miss out on Gods miracle and resulting testimony to his Glory? I think not :-)

We drove home and packed our bags for New York that night with an expectation for a miracle. The day had finally arrived as we arose on the morning of June 20th. My physical condition was a little worse after wrestling with suitcases, back packs, and my guitar the night before. As we prepared to load the car and head to the airport, the phone rang.

The airline was calling to let us know our original itinerary had been cancelled. They rebooked us on later flights, and a completely different route. I hate last minute changes, and made every effort to take control of rebooking our flights. As I was speaking with the agent, Susan was praying that God would be in control instead of me. She came into the bedroom, looked at me and said "Honey, it's a God thing!" and I realized she was right.

We would end up flying to San Francisco later that day, and then a six hour flight to the east coast, on a red eye. The long flight east, would take place when I was usually sleeping under the influence of pain meds. I had also been changed to a window seat, which I never would have booked. God is really smart.

About a half hour before we touched down, I finally woke up. I stood from my "special cushion" enhanced seat, and headed for the rest room. Susan looked at me as I returned to my seat, and asked how I was feeling. She was expecting some pretty serious pain inspired sounds, but they never came. I felt pretty darn good for a guy who hadn't been able to sit for more than a few minutes in the weeks leading up to this trip! I was thankful for God's mercy.

While in New York, I began to notice subtle changes in my condition. I was actually getting better. I had a little less pain, and gained a little more mobility almost every day! We visited with my mom, my sisters, and my friends. I hadn't been that cheerful for months! On our last full day in town, I played a little informal concert at the nursing home where my mom lives. My sisters and a few residents on mom's floor also enjoyed the show.

Then, as we were saying our goodbyes, we received another unsolicited confirmation. My mom's 94 year old roommate Mary, is very hard of hearing. She is a very sweet gal, and has been a good friend to my mom. She also keeps the TV blasting at unthinkable levels, and is often unaware of anything else. Out of the blue that day, above the blaring television, she looked up at me while pointing her finger and said, "Don't you get that back surgery, no surgery!"

The return flight was just as smooth. After returning, I stopped taking all medications prescribed for my back issue. There have been times when the enemy tries to convince me I'm not really healed, but I've learned to resist the attacks and accept my gift of healing. Today I can do everything I used to enjoy before all of this happened. I can even ride off road trails on my mountain bike. Jesus healed me. He's got my back.

He's Our Provider

Susan's parents were blessed with a beautiful ocean front property, on which they lived and worked over forty years. They were also blessed with good health and vitality for most of their lives. After retiring from his accounting business at the age of eighty, Bob and Sarah continued to enjoy life to its fullest. They travelled, spent time with family, and enjoyed their beautiful ocean front home.

They were offered large sums of money for it on several occasions, but knew it was a gift from God. They were able to purchase the property through a series of events only he could arrange, when they had almost nothing to speak of. We never expected them to leave this world any time soon, but in the back of our minds the property was like a security blanket. Bob passed away suddenly at the age of eighty three, and eighteen months later, Sarah joined him in heaven.

There was a reverse mortgage on the property, which had to be paid within a certain period after Sarah passed. Coastal property values in Southern California were at an all-time low, and there wasn't a lot of interest when we listed it. A neighbor who asked to be given first priority, wasn't making any offers either. Each time the asking price was lowered, he was given first priority. When the price was lowered one more time, he was given a final chance, but declined to make an offer.

The mortgage company had already given us two extensions. They told us there would not be another. The deadline was approaching fast, and it looked as though we might lose the property. This would leave the family with no inheritance at all. Finally, we got an offer, but during escrow the title search revealed an easement access issue. The buyer had already fallen in love with the property, and wanted to proceed with the purchase. Escrow closed just in the nick of time. God's time. The family would receive an inheritance.

Bob was a collector of palm trees, and planted hundreds of different varieties on the property. After the sale, Susan and her sister Cheryl were at the house when they noticed a man and two women approaching. There was something different about them. Susan describes them as "beautiful people." The girls invited them inside.

The man asked if the property was still for sale. They told him no, it had finally sold. He asked if they were happy with the selling price. They answered "We wish we could have received a little more." At that, one of the women said something strange. "Would a hug help?" Then they asked to have a look around, and the girls obliged. They were admiring the various palm trees, as if they already knew all about them. To this day, the girls believe it was a visit from above.

Earlier that year, I was laid off from my job of eleven years. At fifty seven, there wasn't a lot of interest in my resume. I needed a job, and all of my leads had fallen through. I was getting pretty discouraged. Susan and I were co-leaders of a small group from church, along with our friends Dan and Peggy. One night I asked the group to pray for a job. As Dan prayed, I felt something powerful in my spirit. When that happens, something good usually follows. The next morning, I received an email from one of my former employers. I had worked there almost twenty years ago. He offered me a job, and I accepted.

Without Susan's inheritance, and my new job, we could have lost our house, our cars, and who knows what else. One of the last things Susan's mom said before leaving this world, was "Jesus is everything." She was right. Security blankets can disappear, but he remains forever. He is our provider. There are so many stories I could share. When I first conceptualized this book, it was all about the miracles. I was thinking, "The Miracle Book." There is one more I would like to share.

Rock the Coach

God cares about the little things too. Last Christmas, Susan and I wanted to get away for a few days in our motor home. We especially love spending time at the beach, and riding our bikes. At our state beaches, camp sites are booked seven months in advance. We had no reservation for the coming holiday weekend. We really wanted to go, and we asked God to make a way. Just two days before the weekend arrived, we checked on line for cancellations. If one came up, it would be taken just as fast as it appeared. As we were searching, an RV site became available and we booked it.

We thanked the Lord and shouted for joy. This was going to be a great holiday weekend. The weather was nice and our site was near the sand with a beautiful ocean view. It's a dry campground, so we needed to manage our electrical power, water supply, and waste tanks. The day before departure, I would normally run the engine and recharge our house batteries. I turned the engine over for several minutes with no luck. It just would not start. I had never seen this before. It always fired right up!

It was two days before Christmas, and we planned to leave the next day. We wanted to get back in time for Christmas Eve services at our church. The waste tanks had to be drained, and we needed time to unload before taking it back to the storage facility. If things went as usual, we could make it happen. I did everything I could to make that engine start. Susan suggested calling the Auto Club and I did. He came to our site and exhausted all of his best trade secrets with no luck. We could arrange for a tow, but decided to stay as planned, and hope for a small miracle the next day.

I tried to stop thinking about it and enjoy our last day at the beach. As I was drifting off to sleep that night, a persistent phrase kept repeating in my head. Rock the coach. When morning came, I had completely forgotten those words. After breakfast, I decided to give it one more try before calling to arrange a tow. It was the day before Christmas, and

I would need to put my request in early. We said a short prayer and I turned the key. No dice. Being towed with full waste tanks, two bikes, and a fully loaded motor home on Christmas Eve was not going to be fun.

As I picked up my phone to make the call, those words came back into my head. Rock the coach. I pondered the phrase, and then asked Susan to humor me for a moment. We stood on opposite sides, placed our hands against the walls, and rocked that coach. After a good ten seconds of rocking, I sat down in the driver seat one more time. I placed the key in the ignition and gave it a twist. Vroom! The engine fired right up! We jumped and shouted for joy, thanking Jesus for his words of wisdom. Rock the coach.

34 - He Has a Plan

If there is one thing we can all agree on, it is this. These bodies are temporary. One year ago, my back was healed as we headed to New York to visit family and friends. We had a great time with my son, his wife and family, my brothers and sisters, my mom, and our friends. In two days, we are going back again. On this trip, we scheduled extra time to spend with our new grandson. We have been anticipating this visit with great joy for months. Today, I received a call from my sister Tina. Mom is hospitalized, and not doing well. In fact, the doctors are giving her one or two weeks to live.

Talk about a mood shift, wow. Only God knows the hour of our departure from this world. Mom is eighty nine years young, and has always been blessed with the ability to bounce back from near death. Lately, I've been calling her "The unsinkable Marion Brown." I don't know exactly what the next few weeks hold for us, but I do know this. God has a plan for all of our lives, and his timing is perfect. I trust him to have my family's best interest at heart. He has never let me down. He hasn't always done things the way I expected, but only he can see the big picture.

My mom has a relationship with Jesus, and she knows that her future is bright. As you know by now, I too have a relationship with Jesus. No matter what happens, my future is good, because he is good. I promised not to preach, and will do my best to keep that promise. I can only tell you what I have seen, and experienced in my life. I am also compelled to tell you this, and I mean it with all my heart.

I want you to experience his love, his joy, his peace, his patience, his kindness, his goodness, his faithfulness, his gentleness, and his self-control. He is the source of all these wonderful things, and he is ready and willing to share them with you. Start the conversation today. Be sincere, tell him how you feel. He always answers my prayers, and I know he will answer yours. My hope is that you will reflect on all you have seen and heard in these pages, and ask yourself what this could mean for you.

May God bless you with his love.

About The Author

Alex Brown is an author and singer-songwriter. He lives in California with his wife of thirty eight years, Susan. They have two married adult children. Waterfalls and Bridges is Alex's first book. Alex released an EP in 2012 titled Four Seasons One God, and released a new CD in 2015 titled Show Some Love.

For more information about Alex's music and books, visit his web site at the following address:

http://www.alexbrownsongs.com

42714744R00105

Made in the USA
Charleston, SC
06 June 2015